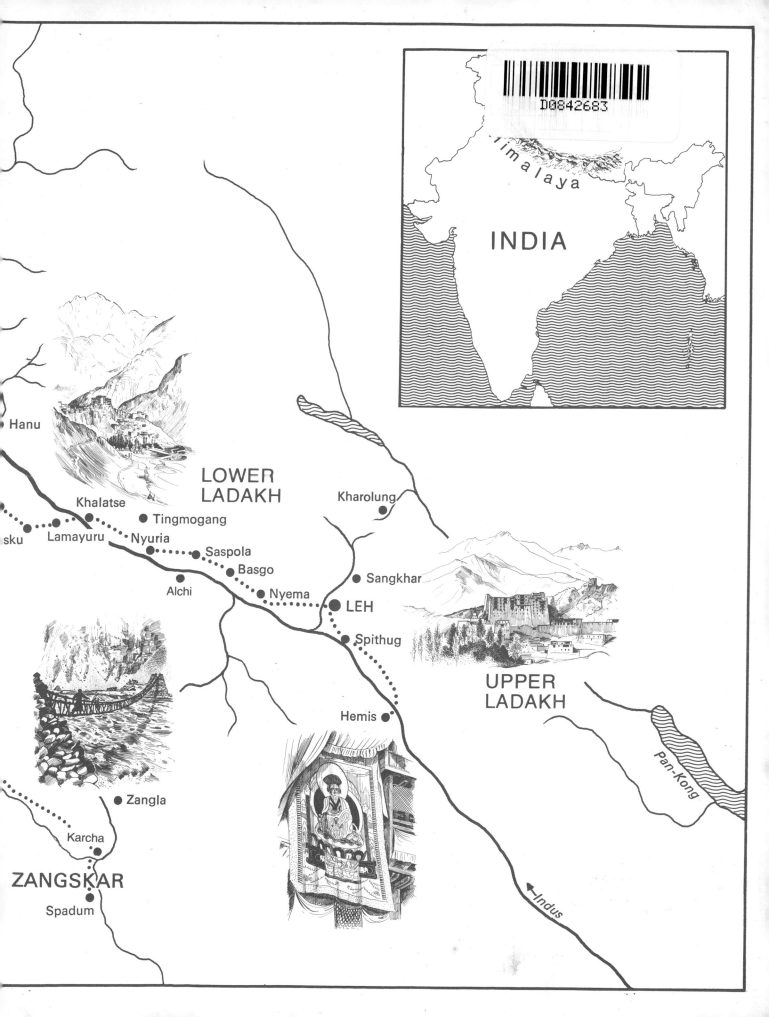

Hanu

LOWER
LADAKH

Kharolung

Khalatse

Tingmogang

sku

Lamayuru

Nyuria

Saspola

Basgo

Alchi

Nyema

Sangkhar

LEH

Spithug

UPPER
LADAKH

Hemis

Pan-Kong

INDIA

Himalaya

ZANGSKAR

Zangla

Karcha

Spadum

Indus

Heinrich Harrer

* Ladakh *

Heinrich Harrer

LADAKH

Gods and mortals
behind the Himalayas

with 154 photographs in colour
and a map.

Pinguin-Verlag, Innsbruck

 The English Book Store
New Delhi

The following two photographs were kindly made available: On page
16 by F. A. Brockhaus Verlag, Wiesbaden; and on page 101, above,
by Dr. Stefan Schlagintweit. All the other photographs were taken by
the author.
Photographs selected and arranged by Jochen Pabst.

Translated by Richard Rickett

1980 edition.
Copyright 1978 by Pinguin Verlag, A-6021 Innsbruck.
All rights reserved.
Printing and binding: Wiener Verlag, Vienna.
Printed in Austria.
ISBN 3–524–76002–3

Contents

Ladakh

Never be in a hurry when exploring the valleys of Ladakh. You can tell the time by how high in the sky the sun is, and the days are like the caravan routes stretching away into the distance as far as the eye can see. Only by "taking it easy" can you learn to appreciate this country.

Ladakh is far too kaleidoscopic to be dismissed with a string of platitudes. Its people, even the meanest peasant, are imbued with a culture handed down from generation to generation for thousands of years. Personally I am in no doubt at all that Ladakh is the most interesting country to visit that one could possibly imagine. It fulfils almost all the expectations of the traveller who is prepared to see it through his own eyes, to experience it through his own emotions, to comprehend it through his own sensibility.

So far, I have visited this wonderful country six times, my first visit being during my escape to Central Tibet in 1944. I fully intend to return there every year and shall be overjoyed as soon as the Indian Government opens up another of Ladakh's valleys, with new people to cultivate and new monasteries to explore. In many of these valleys only the great explorers of old, such as Schlagintweit and Sven Hedin, have set foot. Another thought that keeps urging me to revisit "Little Tibet" is the possibility that international discord may prompt India to close the frontiers again. At the time of writing they are still open and it is only mountain passes completely blocked by snow that cuts the Ladakhis off from the rest of the world throughout the long and bitter winter, when nothing is more important to them than strict religious observance. Once the snow has melted the stream of visitors resumes, but within limits imposed by Nature: some find the altitude too much for them, others are deterred by inadequate standards of transport and accommodation.

Two totally different worlds clash here: western civilisation, with all its technological and scientific achievements, and the ancient world of the Ladakhis, with its religious way of life that ensures internal harmony.

We, with our technical resources, can help these people to preserve their ancient traditions before it is too late. We cannot of course expect them to forgo immediately all the amenities of the twentieth century: the transition must be cautious and gradual, and they should be shown how to preserve their age-old rites and customs, their monasteries and sacred relics. Too often in the course of history have we been far too slow to realise the importance of the past.

I have attempted to portray through photographs one of the loveliest lands on earth, and the chapters will, I hope, elucidate some of the captions which at first may seem rather puzzling. At the same time this book is offered in gratitude for all the kindness and support I have been accorded by the people of Ladakh.

Roads and Bridges

The little house is so unobtrusive that the passer-by might almost miss it at first were it not for the shady courtyard, the wooden first-floor balcony running round all four walls, and the indefinable charm of "colonial" architecture. This particular passer-by, who had been planning his journey to Ladakh in Srinagar, the capital of Kashmir, was suitably excited by the name of the house: "Nedous". For it was in this courtyard that at 5 a. m. on 16 July 1906 the Swedish explorer Sven Hedin had piled his luggage and assembled his porters and animals for his second expedition to Tibet. Twenty-six months later he returned – alone: his comrades had either abandoned him or succumbed to cold and hunger.

Sixty-nine years later almost to the day I followed in Hedin's footsteps as soon as the Indian government had agreed to open up this north-eastern area of India's most northerly Province and had invited me to visit it.

In Svedin's day (1906) travellers had to negotiate primitive tracks and inhospitable passes. Today there is a proper single-track road to Leh, the capital of Ladakh. Supplies are transported by Indian army trucks to the near-by Chinese frontier, and the non-privileged traveller entrusts himself to decrepit old buses that go as far as they can before giving up the ghost. Provided the 4 or 5 metre wide road through the mountains is not blocked by avalanches or landslides there is no difficulty in arriving at "the land beyond the Himalayas" by road.

But the caravans I kept on meeting might well have dated from Hedin's days. And once you leave the "main road" and the river-courses, there are only the ancient nomadic tracks, which can hardly be made out at all on steep slopes, and hair-raising bridges which are often little more than contraptions of osier-shoots and birch twigs (pages 18 + 19). Today's tourist will next be confronted by what Hedin in his book "Transhimalaya" described as follows: "A precarious bridge was the only means of crossing the grey loamy waters of a roaring tributary. One of the mules fell through a hole up to his stomach and we only rescued his load at the very last minute. Later, the bridge was paved with flat stones to make it safer for posterity." We are still in the Moslem part of Kashmir and the slopes are terraced with rice-fields that are watered by streams tumbling down from the Himalayas. But as we make our way up the Indus valley the countryside becomes bleaker and bleaker: the rice gives way first to buck-wheat, then to maize, until eventually the only crop is barley. Instead of mango and walnut trees there are only Himalaya cedars and birch trees that manage to survive even at over 4000 metres above sea-level. At almost every step we encounter flocks of sheep and herds of goats being driven up to the fertile pastures where the last snow is beginning to melt. It is almost as if entire communities were united in a war against Nature: the only signs of life in the villages are women and children and very old men. As one winter ends they collect wood against next year's.

Even in the valley there are pockets of snow, while the Sochi Pass (3,500 metres) is lined by walls of snow 14 metres high. I was held up for several hours by a seemingly endless avalanche that kept blocking the road: fortunately there was a bulldozer to clear this stretch of the road, but on this occasion it was operating a kilometre or two lower down so someone had to go and summon it. The Sochi-La pass (La is the Tibetan word for pass) is the only road link between Srinagar and Leh, and as all Ladakh's supplies come in via this route it is of the utmost importance to keep the road open during the summer: from autumn till late spring it is impassable. Sven Hedin, who crossed the Sochi Pass a good many times, gives an account of a journey in 1906 that is not without dramatic undertones:

"The road from Baltal over the Sochi Pass looked very different this time. In 1902 the whole countryside was snow-covered, and we slid down icy slopes nearly all the way down.

Page 10/11 →
The road from Lamayuru Monastery down to the Indus Valley. As the crow flies, it is a mere 1000 metres, but it takes about 2 hours to negotiate.

9

This time (1906) about 500 workmen were blasting out a new road, their progress being marked by a series of deafening detonations, followed by avalanches of massive boulders that flew by alarmingly close. Slowly and carefully we toiled up over the rough but firm debris of old avalanches, the narrow winding path consisting merely of ruts made by wheeled traffic. Occasionally we came upon rivulets of melting snow, and then after one fairly easy stretch we were confronted by a steep slope beside a wall of rock, and a sort of primitive flight of steps made of transverse logs. To expect fully laden pack-animals to negotiate such a hazard was asking really rather a lot. Every now and then one of them would lose its footing or a mule would almost fall, which would have meant a sheer drop into the foaming torrent far below and no hope of ever finding the unfortunate animal again. From our vantage-point far above the torrent looked no wider than a piece of ribbon. After we had lost several sacks of corn I decided to have each of the animals led by two men".

A glance at the photographs on pages 11 and 12 will give some idea of the sheer drops and ascents and of the immense physical exertions that a visit to Ladakh entailed before the new road was completed. Today there is a tarmac road from Lamayuru Monastery down to the Indus valley, but its course from left to right of the photograph, i. e. down to the Indus valley, is highly deceptive. You would think a child could throw a stone down into the valley, yet the road takes about 2 hours to negotiate in a jeep.

Suddenly tiny specks of green appear in the far distance (page 31); oases in the high mountains, islands of fertility in an arid wilderness of stones and sand. These oases are man-made, for only where the water tumbling down from the mountains is channeled into such hollows can vegetation survive.

The countryside is suffused with a strange light: it is as if Ladakh's mountains were a riot of colour ranging from green to lilac, whereas when you look at it closely the earth varies from yellow to light brown: here and there individual blades of grass survive in the arid waste. From a distance there seem to be millions of blades of grass, lending colour to a landscape that from closer to looks utterly desolate. The slopes are criss-crossed by hundreds of tracks like strips of cloth, and some of them have been hardened by wind and weather into steps. For hundreds of years caravans have passed this way, but as the hungry animals devoured all the vegetation, it grows only where no caravans have ever passed. Water exists, but there is little evidence of it. There is water in the form of snow in the mountains, in the form of ice in remains of avalanches (pages 38/39), and in the form of brooks babbling along narrow valleys which the traveller usually views from far above. Water from the heavens is scarce, Ladakh's record rainfall being no more than 38.1 centimetres per square metre. With only 12.7 centimetres per square metre, Leh is one of the driest capitals in the world. On the other hand, the temperature fluctuates by as much as 40 or 50 degrees Centigrade between summer and winter.

What sort of a country is Ladakh? Is it a land with clearly delineated frontiers, or a Province with a life of its own, or just a jumble of narrow valleys and high plateaus behind the Himalayas? Is it a unified religious community or a clearly defined racial entity?

Books on Ladakh call it by all sorts of different names such as Indian Tibet, West Tibet, or Little Tibet. There are guide-books entitled "Kashmir and Ladakh" although in point of fact Ladakh is a Province of Kashmir. The British explorer Alexander Cunningham terms it "Ladak" or "Kha-pa-chan", whereas the Swede Sven Hedin prefers "Trans-Himalaya" and the Indian F. M. Hassnain "Moonland". Nowadays an "h" is usually tacked on to the final K (Ladakh). But even the most learned geographers fail to agree whether a name that is now completely obsolete should be written "d Mar-yul", meaning "Red Land", after the colour of the monks' robes, or "Mar-Yul", meaning Low-lying Land.

Nowadays, in the late 20th century, Ladakh is the Tibetan Buddhist part of Mohammedan Kashmir, which in turn forms part of predominantly Hindu India. In matters of religion and learning the population of 105,000 look to the Tibetan capital of Lhasa, the one-time residence of the Dalai Lama. A small minority of the population of Kashmir make the pilgrimage to Mecca and dutifully face in its direction when praying. Most Ladakhis are of pure Tibetan origin but speak a different dialect from that spoken in central Tibet. The spoken word is the same as the written one, whereas in High Tibet some letters are not pronounced. As in any inaccessible part of the world a wide variety of dialects have come into being (and survived) in different valleys, and it frequently happens that inhabitants of two valleys barely ten kilometres apart can hardly understand each other.

It is not generally known that even this small country is partitioned. Of its total area of 95,876 square kilometres, nearly 38,000 belong to China. Only 217.3 square kilometres are arable: in other words, 99.6 % of Ladakh is no use to man or beast. A perfect country, one might think, for hermits and Lamas. There are only two cinemas and libraries, only one theatre, and no fire brigade. On the other hand, Ladakh can boast the second highest golf-course in the world, and all the larger villages have a polo-ground and open-air arenas for archery competitions.

Official statistics reveal that only one Ladakhi in seven can read and write, yet the schoolchildren (at any rate) learn to speak three languages, as their mother-tongue is Tibetan, the official language of Kahmir is Urdu, and they are taught Hindi at the explicit request of the Indian Government. No easy schooling for the children, particularly as each of the three languages uses a completely different alphabet.

Ladakh owes its individuality, its air of gentle innocence to natural barriers and deterrents: the Himalayas, the River Indus, and extreme cold and aridity. On each of my five visits I have been agreeably surprised to keep finding a purer version of Tibet than I had ever previously encountered. There is a wise Tibetan saying that is particularly attributable to Ladakh: "If a valley can only be reached by a precipitous pass, only good friends or sworn enemies will make the attempt". Both categories are frequently encountered on the high pass that the Ladakhis call Potu-La, a 4,200 metre pass that makes breathing an ordeal but

opens up one of the finest views in the world: far below is the celebrated Lamayuru Monastery, an osasis of green in a yellow amphitheatre of fossilized clay (page 30).

The first to acquaint Europe with Ladakh was Herodotus. He told of "wondrous ants the size of little dogs" who when building their under-ground habitations struck gold. At about the same time the land was peopled by Tibetan nomads who professed a religion ("Bön") from which the Tibetan form of Buddhism acquired its demonolatry. A little later the first Indian Buddhist missionaries made their way over the Potu-La pass, and their successors, the "Mön", can still be found in Ladakh and can easily be distinguished from other Ladakhis by their outward appearance and the purity of their religion.

The next people to settle were the "Dards" from Gilgit, and they too introduced their own form of Buddhism. Traces of them still survive in some villages.

A clash between demonolatry and Buddhism was inevitable, and it began in about 900 AD. By the 14th century Buddhism had definitely asserted itself, but only after assimilating so many elements of "Bön" that a sort of blend of the two religions emerged. Frequent attempts were made by Lhasa to induce the Ladakhis to return to the purest form of Buddhism, the result being yet another blend. Various Tibetan manuscripts give accounts of how the reformer Tsongkapa attempted to introduce to Ladakh the more austere principles that had already become established in Central Tibet, and so eventually "red" and "yellow" monks compromised on peaceful co-existence while preserving their own brand of Buddhism, thus illustrating two outstanding characteristics of the "people behind the Himalayas", adaptability and obstinacy. The same two qualities come out in an old Ladakh legend. The King's son Sengge, the Vizier's son Trisong, and the son of a wealthy merchant Rabsal, were close

Page 14/15 →

Over the centuries, passing caravans have imprinted a fine network of tracks in layers of sand hardened by wind and weather.

Sven Hedin (1865–1952) was regarded as one of the greatest experts on Ladakh. This great Swedish explorer travelled widely in Ladakh in the early years of the present century and described the country in the three volumes of his "Trans-Himalaya". Hedin used to prepare his expeditions at the Hotel "Nedous" in Srinagar. The hotel is still open and evokes many memories of this great pioneer.

friends. They played the same games, read the same books, and learnt archery from the same teacher. One day, when the three of them were playing on the bank of the Indus and throwing stones into the river, a shoal of fish that had been sleeping under a large stone emerged to protest. The leader of the fish was so big that the three boys vied with each other in trying to stone him to death. Sengge suggested: "Let us hit the fish on the head, because a fish's vital organs are in its head". But Trisong did not agree: "I have always been taught by my mother that a fish's vital organs are in its stomach, and that is where we must hit him". But Rabsal, the youngest of the three, said: "My grandfather is the oldest man in our town and there is nothing he does not know. He once told me that a fish's vital organs are in its tail, so if we want to kill the fish, we must hit him in the tail". A heated argument developed, the three boys began to fight, and the fish quietly swam away. As soon as the boys saw what had happened they laughed, patched up their quarrel and decided to take their problem to the Lama: only he could decide where a fish's vital organs really were. But the Lama was at prayer and was not disposed to concern himself with

mundane affairs for two whole days. So the three boys returned home and agreed to revisit the Lama in two days' time. As the monastery trumpets gave the signal for evening prayer, Prince Sengge requested an ancient retainer to accompany him to the Lama. The two smuggled themselves into the latter's cell, and Sengge prayed to the god Manjusri, while the retainer slipped a gold coin into the Lama's hand. "Your Holiness", said Sengge, "my friends and I cannot agree about whether a fish's vital organs are in its head, its stomach or its tail. In view of my piety and generosity I beg you to state that a fish's vital organs are in its head when I and my two friends return to you in two days". The Lama agreed.

Next morning Trisong presented himself to the Lama, laid at his feet a sword encrusted with magnificent jewels and said: "Your Holiness; we had an argument and I would like to be assured that a fish's vital organs are in its stomach". The Lama smiled and gave a promise.

That same evening Rabsal might have been observed climbing the hill up to the monastery at dusk. He brought the Lama a fine piece of meat wrapped in a skin. "I pray thee, your Holiness", he began: "I must win a bet: when I come to you with my friends, please confirm that a fish's vital organs are in its tail". Again the Lama agreed – and accepted the meat.

When the day of the Lama's answer dawned, the three friends put on their best clothes and repaired to the monastery, folding their hands above their heads as they set foot on the sacred premises. Next, after piously crossing their hands on their breasts, they prostrated themselves till their foreheads touched the ground, and lit candles before a wonderful image of Buddha before entering the presence of the Lama.

Sengge was the first to address the Lama, telling him of the argument about where a fish's vital organs were situated and closing with the request: "Your Holiness, just as the rays of the sun can pick out a seam of gold in stones, so reveal to us the treasure of pure truth, for we would fain escape from the darkness of ignorance". And Trisong said: "Just as a good sword cuts clean with one swift stroke, so reveal us the real truth at a single stroke". And Rabsal said: "Just as impure meat is covered with skin and hair which has to be removed before the meat can be eaten, so canst thou dissect truth from untruth and open our eyes to it".

Now the Lama was a man of infinite tact. Having accepted gifts from all three of them he replied: "Each one of you is right". The three stared at him in amazement: "How can that be?" they asked. The Lama replied: "Simply because there are three kinds of fish in the world: some have their vital organs in their heads, some in their stomachs, and some in their tails". So the Lama avoided hurting any one's feelings, and the three boys were over-joyed. So was the Lama, for had he not received three lavish gifts; a golden coin, a sword encrusted with jewels, and meat for many days?

A King's son, a Vizier's son, and a monk: Ladakh's chequered history abounds in these and many other illustrious figures. There have been Moslem kings ruling over Buddhist subjects, and Buddhist kings ruling over Moslem subjects. When the country was overrun by the Mongols, it was a Mongol leader, Shah Jahan, who came to the assistance of the Ladakhis and repelled the invaders. Later however they returned and forced the King in Leh to pay annual tribute to Lhasa, a practice that survived into the 20th century even though Ladakh had long formed part of the Maharajah of Kashmir's domains. During my stay in Central Tibet I was able to benefit from this state of affairs because part of this tribute consisted of caravan loads of succulent dried apricots which were sold (or given away) in Lhasa.

Wars were incessant in Ladakh, which is why nearly all monasteries as well as secular com-munities were fortified, as shown in the il-lustration on pages 32/33. And in the village of Basgo in the Indus valley there is a castle perched on a rock that the Ladakhis held for three years against the invading Mongols.

People often pass through Ladakh without ever seeing anything except the road, one or two houses by the roadside, and here and there the shrines that in India are called "Stupa". But off the beaten track, perhaps only a kilometre or

Hermann von Schlagintweit-Sakülünski (1826–1882), a native of Munich, was one of five brothers who became famous for their travels and exhaustive researches. No other book contains so much detailed information about Ladakh as his four volumes entitled "Reisen in Indien und Hochasien", published between 1869 and 1880. His collection comprising 14.777 items was acquired by the Ethnological Museums of Berlin and Munich.

two from the main road, there are monasteries full of priceless treasures, ancient frescoes and weather-beaten carvings of astonishing origi-nality. One such monastery is Alchi, half-hidden away amid a labyrinth of chapels in a "Paradise Garden" of green fields alongside the River Indus. It is reached by a zig-zag path that after passing under two great pointed rocks runs along a Mani wall and then drops down to a green oasis on the other side of the River Indus. Another fine example is Shergo Monastery near Mulbe. A white wall studded with windows clings like a swallow's nest to a rock about 15 metres from the ground. No steps, no ladders: nothing. From the road a steep path leads over acres of stones up to the foot of the rock, to a point where the visitor has the monastery directly above him. To quote a guide-book: "... in keeping with the propor-tions of the monastery, it is inhabited by only two monks, who are looked after by a nun. Some of the rooms, the kitchen for instance, are hewn out of the rock and are more like caves than human habitations".

It is not difficult to understand the enthusiasm with which a British doctor who found himself in Ladakh around the turn of the century

A primitive bridge over the River Sangskar, a precarious contraption of osier shoots, birch twigs and rope.

described his impressions. He started his journey from Srinagar to Leh on horseback, but after covering only a few kilometres dismounted, sat on a stone and wrote in his diary: "Directly in front of me is a cluster of hills of soft sandstone. Behind me is a towering range of mountains culminating in jagged pinnacles silhouetted against an azure sky. As one follows the winding path past the reddish-brown elevations and into the villages, the weird formations of the sandstone foothills gradually occupy the entire foreground. Their bizarre outlines are due to the ceaseless action of wind, rain and snow, producing grotesque formations like prehistoric villages or castellated fortresses, relics of some bygone civilisation".

For the "bizarre" scenery the writer finds correspondingly bizarre words, and concludes: "Even the inhabitants are as completely at one with the landscape as birds or wild animals. It is difficult to identify a distant coolie, even when he is walking along a road. His colourless, homespun clothes, his headgear, even his face (which seems to be as infrequently acquainted with water as the surrounding countryside) are permeated with the dry dust of the desert. Only by his movements can he be distinguished from the grey boulders and the brown sand; unlike the red-clad Lamas, who can be identified from far off, the clarity of the atmosphere affording a visibility that would be beyond the capacity of the human eye in our native land. Yet it is extremely difficult to distinguish a heap of stones from a seated figure. Approaching what we thought was a heap of stones, we peered at it, and suddenly it rose to its feet with the word "m'a-ches" (matches).

During my escape from the British internment camp at Dera Dun I had a curious experience in East Ladakh: after travelling at 3000 to 5000 metres above sea level I showed no visible traces of perspiration. This was all the more unaccountable in that while the shade temperature was only 10° C, in the sun it was over 30° C. Why? The air is so dry that perspiration immediately evaporates. The salt and the fluid that the body loses have to be constantly replaced. One notices this first in one's lips: during a day's march they become very dry, then crack and contract.

The fact that Ladakh's highest road, the "Beacon Highway", is at present closed for strategic reasons is a blessing in disguise as far as tourists are concerned, because between the Nubra Valley and the Chinese frontier it runs at an altitude of 5606 metres above sea-level. As a road-sign just outside Leh puts it, it is "the world's highest road, high enough for the traveller to enjoy a conversation with God". So what with one thing and another, travelling in Ladakh is an adventurous undertaking, especially in the Sangskar valley in the south of the country. Very wisely, the Indian Government opened up the whole district piecemeal, one small area at a time. In the first year, 1974, tourists were only allowed to visit Leh, but in 1976 they were also permitted to enter Sangskar. I was one of the first to visit this tiny kingdom between the Himalayas and the Karakorums and I noted in my diary: "Wonderful cloud-patterns casting shadows over fields of ripening corn and barley. The sky is full of birdsong and radiant morning sunshine. After sharing my frugal breakfast with Norbu, the King's son, I am urging the other members of the caravan to get moving. The fields are already hives of activity, peasants tilling the soil, and sheep, goats and donkeys cropping shoots of barley undisturbed. Against the background af an almost perpendicular wall of rock is the familiar sight of monks drawing water. What a shot for a film, the red-cowled monks hurrying along the grey pathway up the mountainside!" During that visit I had gone on ahead to take photographs. I was able to take close-ups of the children playing in the street because they didn't know what I was doing, but just stared at me. The women were much more on their guard, hiding wherever they could without taking their eyes off me for a second. I passed by massive prayer walls and old Stupas which blended so naturally into the surrounding scenery that they almost seemed to form part of it: the Tibetans have always been very good at complementing the works of nature with the works of man. They have tamed the wilderness and embellished it with cultural monuments that have a curiously comforting effect.

I had not gone far before I came upon a begging trick, a piece of hide held down on the road by stones in the hope that a passer-by would leave a coin or two or a gift of some kind. The beggars themselves invariably remain invisible, hidden behind bushes or walls. I tossed a few sweets and biscuits on to the hide and presently spotted two young shepherd-girls creeping cautiously out of their hiding-place to see what I had left them.

In recent years, tourism has opened up areas that up to a few years ago only explorers could have envisaged. Yet there are still remote corners of the earth where one feels as if one were on another planet, and Sangskar is one of them. Nowhere have I seen so many roses in full bloom – light red roses, dark red roses, yellow roses – interspersed with fragrant tamarisks. In those days (November 1976) the tiny mountain-girt Kingdom of Ladakh could only be reached by mule-tracks, so we assembled a caravan of 14 horses at Panikhar, distributing their loads so as to leave two horses free to carry me and my companion. In this part of Ladakh the mountains rise to a height of 7 135 metres, and even in midsummer the traveller is likely to be surprised by distinctly unpleasant obstacles. Crossing the Pontse Pass, for instance, we were met head-on by a raging blizzard, and the horses were frequently up to their girths in snow. Nothing had changed for a hundred years, since Sven Hedin's day. He must have experienced the same feeling of exhilaration and relief as I did when after crossing the Pontse Pass one of our guides offered me a cup of tea and I crawled into my sleeping-bag in front of a blazing fire in my tent.

Next morning we found ourselves stranded: the horses had bolted during the night and a mare had given birth to a foal. It was after midday before the missing animals were rounded up, and all the fuss about the foal died down. Five days later we came to Sangla, the residence of the Kings of Sangskar. Just before we reached it we had come to a ramshackle bridge over the River Sangskar that was so precarious that it even swayed in the wind. It was enough to daunt even the most intrepid traveller, while as for the animals, nothing would induce them to set foot on it.

Seeing that every traveller in Ladakh has to risk his life over one of these precarious contraptions at one time or another, it may be as well to offer a brief description of them. They can be of two kinds: one kind consists simply of three loosely knotted ropes, one to walk on and two to hold on to. The other kind consists of a log spanning a river, but only projecting beyond the banks by 30 to 40 centimetres on either side, and held in position by four smallish rocks. The "bridge" over the River Sangskar originally consisted of two ropes of osier shoots and birch twigs attached to two stones rooted firmly in the earth: later the Government had the structure strengthened by a wire rope. Underfoot were bundles of twigs fastened to the lateral ropes at intervals of about a metre. The "bridge" sagged so alarmingly that crossing it was like climbing down a ladder at one end and up again at the other. In many cases sections of the middle rope were missing: probably it had just worn through and never been replaced. The middle rope is sometimes so loose and narrow that one needs the self-assurance of a tight-rope walker to maintain a foothold while one's hands grope blindly for the side ropes, which are rough enough to draw blood: gloves are definitely advisable.

Confronted by this "bridge" our cook, who was from Leh, broke out into a cold sweat, whereas the locals trotted across it like squirrels, sometimes even carrying their terrified donkeys across their shoulders, after taking the precaution of tying their legs together, in case the animals panicked and fell into the water, dragging their owners with them.

When the British explorer Dr. Alexander Gerard was travelling in Ladakh in August 1839 to collect material for books and lectures he had to cross a 56 metre-long bridge of woven osier-shoots over the River Ravi near Mahila: in his notebook he classified it as "not safe". For a lecture to the Asiatic Society of Bengal he noted: "It is a curious phenomenon that when you pass trees, houses and fields in a coach you feel as if they are moving past while the coach is standing still. On one of these bridges it is exactly the opposite: the bridge seems to be moving while the torrent below is stationary". The British were the first to make a scientific survey of Ladakh, recording average tem-

Page 22
*Pilgrims in the desert.
After crossing the River
Indus (foreground) they
are making their way to
Alchi Monastery behind
the hills in the
background.*

*A ramshackle old bus
on the way up to
Sochi-La. This pass
crosses the main range
of the Himalayas.*

peratures, details of body temperatures, and the deposits of gold in the bed of the River Indus. They also tried to find out how Herodotus and Megasthenes hit on their stories about "giant ants" striking gold: could these creatures have been marmots? The Germans have also been closely associated with Ladakh: the first missionary was a German; it was Germans who compiled the first Ladakhi dictionary; and all subsequent visitors to Ladakh have relied on the accounts of the five Schlagintweit brothers and availed themselves of the works of the Saxon missionary Jäschke. In some villages even a German word has survived: a child playing with a doll can often be heard muttering the word "Puppe".

Monasteries and Countryside

Ladakh is the land of monasteries par excellence. There is one in almost every village, either a glorified residential building or a miniature fortress perched on a rock high up in the mountains. The number of monks they house ranges from 2 to 100 or more. Some belong to the "red-cap" sect, others to the "yellow-caps", and all owe allegiance to an "incarnation", who is seldom resident. Yet the total number of monks in Ladakh is not very great: although no official figures were included in the 1971 census, estimates vary from 15,000 to 17,000, plus 100 nuns.

For the monks, the monasteries are places of meditation; for tourists, repositories of art-treasures; and for lovers of beauty just part of the scene, for against their background of mountains and valleys they seem like works of man complementing the works of Nature. I cannot imagine a more beautiful or harmonious architectural entity than Lamayuru Monastery (page 30), a more spectacular palette of colours than around the abandoned hill-top fortress near Alchi Monastery, (pages 32 + 33), or a more impressive array than the domes, pinnacles and turrets of the dilapidated monastery of She at the foot of a rock basking in the full glory of the morning sun.

Lamayuru Monastery, though less important than Hemis Monastery 44 kilometres east of Leh, is the oldest monastery in the country and was permitted to harbour criminals seeking sanctuary. Not only is Lamayuru Ladakh's oldest monastery, it is also the largest, as can be appreciated from the main entrance (about 15 minutes from the main road). Its chequered history is a conglomeration of holy legends, myths, and attempts to explain natural phenomena in terms of divine Providence.

In the courtyard, the visitor is given an 8-page booklet, bound in pink paper and dated 11th February 1975, outlining the history of the monastery. "In ancient times, when Sakyamuni Buddha was still living among us and his enlightened teaching in Jambudvipa was spread far and wide, parts of the northern plateau known as Tibet were still uninhabited, and the Lamayuru valley, above which the celebrated monastery now stands, comprised a limpid lake inhabited by sacred snakes known as Nagas. After the Nirvana of Tathagata, Arahat Madhyantaka, a disciple of Ananada, came to this valley and set foot on a small island in the middle of the lake. After performing some miracles and exploring the lake from end to end he foretold that a monastery would be built here in the not too distant future, and made offerings of barleycorn and water to the Nagas. After this ceremony, he dropped the barleycorn into the water and also willed the lake to dry up at one end.

After his departure almost the whole of the lake did dry up and at the foot of a small hill the mud hardened into figures like lions, which is why the hill is still called "Lions' Hill". The barleycorn that Arahat had dropped into the water was shaped by the receding water into a wonderfully beautiful pattern, and in due course the barleycorn shoots grew into a Yungtung (swastika) of grey rye, so that to this day Lamayuru Monastery is know as the Yungtung Gompa, the swastika monastery.

Time passed, and still no human being discovered this wonderful spot until the 10th century A. D., when a celebrated holy man of Buddha named Naropa arrived here, built himself a small hut and passed many years in meditation. Meanwhile Buddhism had become established in Tibet and had also set foot in Ladakh and Gilgit. Scribes from Tibet, especially Rinchen Sangpo, contributed many precious embellishments to the Buddhist Tripitakas, until his fame spread to the four corners of Tibet; and for the King of Ladakh he built no fewer than 108 monasteries, one of them being Lamayuru. Rinchen Sangpo's design consisted of a central building and four ancillary ones, one at each

Page 26/27 →
A village near Lamayuru Monastery. Its inhabitants are entirely dependent on the monks and pay them tribute in the form of part of the harvest. The circular formations on the slopes (right) serve as threshing-floors.

Page 28/29 →
The Loess near Lamayuru Monastery looks like a rough sea of corrugated tawny earth.

*Left
Lamayuru. A narrow
path leads up to the
monastery and the
village at its foot.
The loess in the
background resembles
the backcloth of a
gigantic theatre hewn
out of the foothills.*

*Oases in the desert:
the green islets amid
a desolate expanse of
brown sand and
stones are a sure sign
of water.*

corner of the main building. As time went on the central building was enlarged until it assumed the proportions of the present monastery. Of the four other buildings only fragments remain, but one of them, on the west side of the monastery, contains some original frescoes which are unfortunately in a very bad state of preservation.

As soon as the monastery was completed some 400 monks moved in, and an abbot, a Kadampa Lama, was appointed from Central Tibet. The Kadampas are a numerous sect founded by Acharya Dipankara Srinjana, and their tradition survived for six centuries.

For the last ten years of the 16th century Ladakh was ruled by the virtuous King Jamyang Namgal, who built a great many roads and canals as part of the comprehensive scheme for expanding the country's trade. On one occasion, when he was hiring labourers to make a canal near Hemis, a seps the size of a full-grown man came out of a cave in the hillside and was promptly put to death by the workmen with their spades. But the seps turned out to have been a Naga, who took revenge on the king by afflicting him with leprosy. Neither his doctors nor the lamas could cure him, but then somebody recalled an ancient prophecy, and the great Lama Dhanmatsang of the Brigunpa sect was summoned to Ladakh. The Lama left his cave on Mt. Kailas, exorcised the spirit of the giant seps, and after a day or two the king was not only fully restored to health but even showed his gratitude by offering the Lama his kingdom. Eventually it was agreed that monasteries should be built in Ladakh, and the king presented the Lama with Lamayuru monastery. He furthermore decreed that Lamayuru should be exempt from taxes and independent of the law of the land. It was also declared a place of asylum where even the most desperate criminals could enjoy sanctuary within a mile of its precincts. This is why Lamayuru is also known as "Tharpa Ling", meaning "place of liberation". As time went on a number of villages came into being round the monastery, and in each village there was a subsidiary monastery, from which from time to time monks came to the main monastery at Lamayuru for meditation, especially on special occasions, the most important being the second month of the Tibetan year, the recitation of the holy scriptures taking place in the fifth year, a pattern which is still observed today. The gayest and most elaborate festival is the New Year, when the Lamas put on a sort of three-day ballet in masks and costumes. This spectacle attracts thousands of Ladakhis from all parts of the country to a great foregathering in the courtyard of the monastery.

Some 20 or 30 monks reside permanently at Lamayuru, sunk in prayer, meditation, and the holy scriptures. Although the monastery owns some land, it depends for its existence on donations by the faithful. It is also an essential part of the ancient Himalaya civilisation. Its influence is paramount in the propagation of the Buddhist religion, which is unique in that it helps people to live in peace and harmony and enables them to attain the final status of a Buddha.

Many incarnations live in Ladakh, but the head of all the monks is His Holiness Drugpa Rinpoche of Hemis monastery. His "second in

Page 32/33
An abandoned fortress near Alchi Monastery. The predominant colours in the more fertile regions of Ladakh are green, ochre, yellow and dark brown.

Page 34/35
On the way from Leh to Hemis Monastery, with the morning sun playing on a splendid array of towers, pinnacles and stone-terraces.

Page 36/37
On the roof of Tiktse Monastery a young monk points towards Tibet across the gradually widening Indus valley.

Page 38/39
Between the Sochi Pass and the village of Dras: remains of an avalanche left over from winter.

Page 40
The monastery near Mulbe was built by monks at the foot of a rock resembling a phallus.

command" is Togden Rinpoche, under whose guidance Lamayuru is conscientiously discharging its duties as a Buddhist mission.

The view from the roof of the monastery shows how closely the welfare of the monks is bound up with that of the peasants. In the little village situated at the bottom of a slope, (pages 26 + 27) one can clearly see how the houses adjoin small caves as a protection against winter storms. On the circular formations in the right half of the picture grain is threshed by animals plodding in monotonous and leisurely circles, and the peasantry pay tithes in the form of part of the harvest. Such greenery as there is is encroached upon by darkish brown masses of rock and stones, yet greenery does manage to thrive where water can be made available, as on the left of the picture. Without water, the earth is barren. One of the most spectacular features of Lamayuru is the yellow semi-circle surmounting the monastery like a gigantic backcloth hewn out of the foothills. According to the legend, it was here that the water receding from the dried-up lake at the command of Arahat Madhyantaka solidified (pages 28 + 29). The nearer one approaches this mass of loess, the stronger grows the impression of a vast expanse of petrified waves, their crests glinting under the noonday sun.

For 150 years Lamayuru has left travellers at a loss for words. No wonder the British doctor and missionary R. Reeve Heber wrote in his book "Himalayan Tibet and Ladakh (1903)": "How can one possibly describe this focal point of this fantastic land? This landscape of purple hills, snow-clad peaks and a dark blue sky, does it not create an impression of some gigantic hand having exposed to the noonday sun something that has been hidden in the bowels of the earth since time immemorial?" Sven Hedin alone seems to have been not particularly impressed by the monastery, monks and surroundings of Lamayuru, and contented himself with observing that "the stony elevation on which the monastery is built rises almost perpendicularly from the plain. One or two white temples stand out against the ubiquitous grey of their environment, and at the bottom of the valley there is some arable land between far from luxuriant clumps of trees."

Monks also play an important part in the social life of Ladakh, for as well as to their religious observances they devote themselves to education, irrigation, and the preservation of ancient medical lore. Until quite recently at least one member of any family lived and worked in a monastery, and this must still be so, seeing that of a total population of 105,000 some 1,700 are monks.

I have had the pleasure of following in the footsteps of the aforesaid A. Reeve Heber, who 74 years before me visited Sangskar monastery, only 8 kilometres from Leh. From previous experience in Tibet I know that with few exceptions all the monasteries are built to the same design, a design that Heber devotes 9½ pages to, describing it in the minutest detail. It was in July 1975 that I followed in his footsteps through the small side-door into the courtyard: *"In the middle of the courtyard was a high pole of poplar wood with a yak's tail flying from the top of it, and a prayer-banner reaching to the ground".*

I was greeted by the barking of dogs, which accord the same treatment to all visitors, friend or foe. The massive wooden main gate was firmly closed. Near it was the abbot's mounting-block. Entering the monastery by the main gate one comes immediately upon the main temple, which is three stories high and delineated by a layer of ochre logs of equal length. From its roof waved a splendid array of prayer-banners. The windows are like miniature balconies, garishly painted and decorated with material in the colours of the five elements. The other sides of the courtyard are lined with two-story buildings which serve as the monks' living-quarters. I noticed that the doors and windows are not in a straight line, either because the floors are not quite level, or because the windows are at different heights. Up a flight of steps I came to a sort of ante-room leading to the refectory.

"On the left-hand wall is a painting of the wheel of life supported by a sort of dragon. The wheel comprises three circles, the innermost one being divided into six sectors, and three creatures – a dove, a snake and a pig – symbolising the three vices which hold Man fast to the wheel: lust, anger, and stupidity".

The air in the refectory was heavy with incense, and such dim light as there was came either from the door through which we had just entered, or through a slit in the ceiling. Heavy hangings and pillars of dark wood accentuated the darkness of the room. On an elevated seat immediately opposite the door sits the prayer-leader with his legs crossed under him, and immediately in front of him is a small table. The monks sit on two rows of benches between the pillars. At the back of the room I could just make out the contents of the monastery liberary reposing in dusty bookcases.

Behind the prayer-leader one of the monks opened a small door through which we passed into a room full of a bizzarre variety of different objects – models of temples like dolls' – houses, statues of Buddha, copper ewers and butter-lamps (the wick is steeped in butter instead of oil). This room led into two more rooms and finally into a room full of valuable Thangkas (religious subjects painted on silken banners). A sixth room containing ancient frescoes is only used for special ceremonies during the first month of the Buddhist year. By way of a staircase so steep that it was more like a ladder I reached the room allocated to the prayer-leader and his assistant. The furnishing included well-cushioned chairs, and little 40 centimetres high Tibetan tables for books and oil lamps. On one of the walls hung a demon's mask.

"We enter a room in which there is a huge statue of a god named 'Dukar': it is so big that its head surmounts the two stories of the building, which is why the monks have superimposed a sort of penthouse. We climbed up to it and enjoyed a marvellous view of the Kardong Pass and Leh".
Finally we were shown the monastery kitchen, which was rather small and not very high. There were slits in the roof to allow the smoke to escape and through them we could see strips of blue sky. Bundles of thorns gathered by lay helpers were stacked by the door: wood is too expensive to be used for heating, and thorns, though they burn very fast, give out a tremendous heat. A stew of lumps of flour, fat and turnips was bubbling away in huge earthenware vessels. The cooks and their assistants looked positively unearthly when they fleetingly emerged covered in soot from dense clouds of smoke or when the whole kitchen was suffused in a ruddy glow from the blazing fire. Every now and then young boys who had just left home to take up residence in the monastery tipped some of the stew into smaller vessels, which were then served to the monks in the refectory.

"We were full of admiration", concludes Heber, "as we left the monastery and made our way back to Leh through fields lined with fleurs de lis just as the sun was setting over the mountains and lighting our way home".

The scenery looks as if it had been specially designed for this religion. Or could this religion only survive in a landscape like this? It is astonishing how peaceful Ladakh seems, considering that the landscape displays every aspect of savagery. Perhaps this impression of peace and quiet is due to the Ladakhis having adapted themselves to the scenery or having been constrained by Nature to build as Nature builds. Even in places where the works of man have decayed, the ruins do not obtrude. She monastery for instance, east of Leh, from whatever angle one looks at it, seems never to have been built by human hand but simply to have come into being. (pages 34/35). The temples and houses are organically integrated into their natural surroundings, yet Man has made vital contributions to this synthesis of architecture and Nature. The water, for instance, which flows down from the Kardong Pass when the snow melts in spring, never reaches the River Indus but is diverted by the peasants to irrigate their fields.

The visitor to Ladakh should take his time and never be in a hurry. Almost every monastery has its own special festival or possesses some work of art of striking originality. There are at least nine monasteries on, or at least not far off, the beaten track: Mulbe, Lamayuru, Ridzong, Alchi, Likir, Pyang, She, Thiktse and Hemis. The great festival at Hemis is in June or July, and at Thiktse usually in December.

The largest monastery in Ladakh is Karcha, just above the point where the Rivers Pontse and Kargyas unite to form the River Sangskar. Its head is Ngari Rinpoche, the younger brother of the Dalai Lama. The very fact that part of it is in ruins enhances its value as a discovery. Above it are ruins af an ancient building which was abandoned centuries ago and originally served as a vantage-point where beacons were kindled to warn other monasteries of the approch of Moslem forces, the arch-enemies. Entering Karcha I passed under two Stupa gates with magic circles inscribed on their ceilings. The little temple was full of tattered Thangkas and some ancient statues crawling with flies. On the other hand the walls were newly decorated, and a number of Thangkas on view in the refectory testified to the wealth of hidden treasures in the monastery's possession. With characteristic prudence the monks have preserved behind glass a particularly valuable figure of the "God of Grace", of whom the Dalai Lama is a reincarnation. On top of the building are three stupas almost touching each other (page 132), each with a wooden pole for flying prayer-banners.

Just as the Ladakhis rob nature of her water, so visitors have discarded the old geographical rames, most of which had a definite and picturesque meaning. What was once "Senge Kabab" ("he that flees from the lion's revenge") is now the River Indus, and the "Lanche Kabab" ("he that flows from the elephant's mouth") has become the River Salech. The Bramaputra was originally "from the horse's mouth", and the familiar "Darjeeling" is a corruption of "Dordche Ling", "garden of the thunderbolt". Not even the Tibetan section of the Himalayas has been able to preserve its original name of "Ri-gyal", the "country of the mountain-kings".

Tibetan proverbs, on the other hand, are still current, and have either found their way into other languages or been adapted to Ladakhi requirements. Another survival is the ancient custom of celebrating the beginning of new year twice, once in Ladakhi and once in Tibetan style, the latter being the official one. This practice originated when King Jamja ("Sweet harmony") decided to invade the neighbouring Kindom of Purig and consulted his astrologers about the most suitable day to launch his attack. The soothsayers opined that no day could be considered suitable for making war and advised the king to wait until the New Year Festival, whereupon the king decided to advance the aforesaid festival by two months. He therefore went to war against Purig in December and January instead of in March and was (not surprisingly) taken prisoner. But his innovation of a double New Year Festival has survived him by over 300 years.

Men and Beasts

It is extremely difficult to form an overall impression of the Ladakhis simply by observing the numerous tribes that make up this relatively small community. Yet these tribes, some of them restricted to just one or two villages, do throw highly interesting light on a blood-soaked history, and on a present-day way of life which has preserved a number of traditions that are puzzling even to those who abide by them.

The adventurous German explorer Hermann Schlagintweit (who was given the nickname "Sakülünski" after climbing Mt. Kuelün in 1864) was guilty of over-simplification when he wrote in his "Reisen in Indien und Hochasien": "Like the inhabitants of the whole of Gnari Khorsum and of the domains of the Dalai Lama, the people of Ladakh are purely Tibetan, extending in the northern part of Ladakh, in Nubra, as far as the watershed frontier of the Karakorums. In the rest of Ladakh this racial purity was contaminated by the arrival of Islam. Even 40 to 50 English miles west of Le there are a great many Moslems."

The first Christian missionary in Ladakh, a German named Wilhelm Heyde of the Moravian sect, described the Tibetans' "slit eyes, protruding cheek-bones, smooth black hair and brown skin as typical Mongolian features. There are also a number of tribes of mixed origin descended from early Hindu immigrants from India. One quality all these tribes have in common is a total disregard of cleanliness. The older people never bath, and the younger people do so only very occasionally in summer. As a general rule, only the hands and face are ever washed, and only the well-to-do wear shirts. Not unnaturally, bugs of all kinds are ineradicable elements of the population".

After reading European books, an Indian expert on Ladakh, Prof. F. M. Hassnain, posed the question whether washing is an essential feature of civilisation: perhaps the Ladakhis had attained a higher level of spiritual realisation by attaching more importance to water with prayer than to water with soap?

In such a cold, dry and inhospitable land only a people of exceptional stamina, ingenuity, toughness, fortitude and adaptability could hope to settle and prosper. Only a religion "made to measure" like Tibetan Buddhism could survive: Christianity never became established here.

The Ladakhis are a community of peasants, craftsmen and seasonal nomads living at from three to five thousand metres above sea-level in oases they have themselves created out of melting snow and glaciers. They have evolved a complicated system of irrigation to water their lucerne and barley fields. Their houses are built of bricks of dried clay or dung, and their children wear hand-woven clothes. In summer, they conduct their flocks and caravans up to the high plateaus which they irrigate naturally (and therefore better), and cross high mountain ranges by tracks left by their predecessors; in doing so they are motivated not by lawlessness or pure selfishness but by a sense of duty to the community. The shepherds in charge of thousands of animals deliver butter, wool and other vital raw materials, and the caravan-leaders, though far from prepossessing in appearance, (pages 54 + 58) constitute links between the uplands and the lowlands, between those who keep themselves alive and those who keep others alive.

The inhabitants of this land behind the Himalayas have achieved something that to other peoples still remains only a dream: they have made the wilderness fertile. For this they have been, and still are, willing to make social sacrifices, and only by evincing a highly developed community spirit have the Ladakhis been able to live off their environment.

There are to all intents and purposes only two seasons in Ladakh: a short, torrid summer and a long, icy winter. For six or seven months of the year the country lies under a blanket of snow; but as soon as the snow starts to melt (usually in May), the earth awakes from its long winter sleep. Behind his wooden plough (page 62) drawn by yaks or dzos (a cross between a yak and an Indian ox) the peasant sows his seeds, irrigates his land, weeds it and waits. The harvest is two months later; and by about 15 September oxen and donkeys are busy threshing. As well as water, wind comes as a boon to scatter the chaff.

The winter, which lasts from November to

May, is devoted to weaving and spinning, to putting to good use what has been harvested during the summer, and to making what will be needed for the following summer.

It is not easy to converse with Ladakhis because they speak a dialect which though clearly of Tibetan origin differs appreciably from all other languages. In the words of the Swiss travellers Pierre Jaccard and Pierre Vittoz: "A European vocabulary bears very little resemblance to that used by the Ladakhis, because their daily life, their interests, their upbringing and their civilisation have nothing in common with European standards. To take just one example: to us, the word 'crockery' denotes fragile objects, whereas to the Ladakhis it means something solid and durable, because their 'crockery' is made of silver or copper. Similarly, their Tibetan dialect, though rich in nouns, is almost totally lacking in generic or abstract expressions. For example, the Ladakhis have a different word for every kind of tree or wood, but no word for 'tree'. Consequently one has to express oneself with the utmost precision, specifying 'willow', 'poplar', or 'juniper'. The same applies of course to all pursuits which figure prominently in the Ladakhis' way of life. They have enough words connected with horses to fill a whole dictionary. There are some thirty different words for describing a horse's exact colour, and a separate word for each piece of harness, yet there is no word for 'riding' or 'saddle'".

The first settlers here were definitely Tibetan nomads with sheep, goats and yaks. Their successors can still be encountered in Changtang, ten days' journey from Leh. They dwell in black tents made of yak-hair with a slit in the top to allow the smoke to escape (even inside their tents they cook on an open fire). The next arrivals were the Indian Buddhist missionaries who introduced red robes: their descendants ("Mön") are now scattered all over Ladakh. From time immemorial these "Mön" have been joiners, musicians and drummers, and even today there are still considerable difficulties over a "Mön" marrying a "Bö-pa" (Tibetan). After the "Mön" came the "Dards" from the Moslem Hunza district, and they too have retained a good deal of their individuality. They are Aryans and live mostly near Dras and

Gorkon, and it is they who introduced polo to Ladakh. Today they are know as Drogpas, a word denoting nomads in Ladakh and Tibet. In the village of Podrang, the other side of the 5099 metre Chang Pass (Chang means 'north'), one finds the first outposts of Changpas, a people with Mongolian eyes and flat noses: their hair is either loose or plaited (page 58, left). Their clothing consists of long coats and red boots with extraordinarily thick soles. Their tents are only about 1½ metres high and open at the top. They use their sheep as beasts of burden which can carry up to 15 kilograms. They also carry salt to Leh market, where they are usually sold along with their loads. The Khampas, who as their name implies come from the East Tibetan Province of Kham, had to abandon their nomadic existence when the Chinese closed the frontier. Doubts as to whether this made much difference to them are expressed by the English explorer Heber in his book "Himalayan Tibet and Ladakh": "they are on the move through the Himalayas in such numbers that one wonders whether there are still any Khampas left in Kham itself. At all events their nickname of the 'gypsies of the West Tibet' is amply justified.".

Last, but not least, there are the Baltis from the Province of Baltistan north-west of Leh: they are Moslems and were often at war with Ladakh before becoming part of it. Today the Province belongs to Pakistan, but the Baltis still climb up to Leh when there is trade to be done. All these tribes and nomadic peoples, while causing considerable confusion with remarkable consequences, have also bequeathed a legacy which their descendants have not known how to exploit.

The Drogpas living in the villages of Hanu and Da north of Lamayuru monastery started their nomadic existence in Gilgit and ended up by embracing Buddhism, though there are still families who allow at least one of their number to "go over" to Islam. Dr. A. H. Francke, the greatest expert on Ladakh, came upon families in which the older generation were Buddhists and the younger Moslems.

In the village of Khalatse the people say prayers that everyone knows by heart but nobody understands, because they include words from the Dard language that died out a long time ago.

Many Drogpas have to eschew eggs, others eat no fish. Heber discovered a third class of Drogpas who observed a singular custom that I have not personally been able to confirm, families eating together though one of them was a Moslem and the rest were Buddhists. Obviously some way had to be devised of separating the various kinds of meat in the pot. Buddhists were allowed to eat animals that had been shot or killed by, say, a blow on the head, but Moslems were not, for the Koran lays down that animals must be slaughtered by having their throats cut to the word "Bismillah" (it is the will of Allah). So what the family did was to place in the pot a piece of wood with the magic property of separating clean from unclean flesh: all the Moslem had to do was to be careful to eat from "his" side of the wooden partition.

In the summer of 1975 I was crossing the Potu Pass when I saw a Ladakhi riding a diminutive horse: he was wearing a typical felt hat at a rakish angle, and round his neck was a chain of bone-beads. With a gesture with which I was familiar from Tibet he slightly raised his hand and put his tongue out – the politest greeting he knew. Later, I met a similar individual (and horse) at Leh market (page 49): he had travelled miles with a load of dried yak-dung in his saddle-bags in the hope of selling it as fuel. On the way to Lamayuru monastery I encountered a young girl collecting yak-dung in a basket and leading her little sister by the hand. She was extremely shy and at first made no response to my Tibetan words of greeting. It was only with some sweets that I eventually overcame her shyness, and she told me she was 19 and still unmarried. She also agreed to carry the heavy batteries of our film camera (we were shooting a TV film) down to the monastery and back for one rupee.

On the way to Sangskar I came upon a phenomenally ill-favoured female standing in the middle of a field with her arms above her head and every now and then uttering fearsome shrieks. It was a human scarecrow (page 54), paid by her village to keep crows off their newly-sown fields. On her left wrist was a bracelet of shells that she had been given in childhood: now that she had "grown into it", so to speak, she would never be able to get it off except by breaking it.

It was market-day in Leh, and in addition the great mystery-play at Hemis monastery was attracting visitors from all over Ladakh. We encountered beings who seemed to belong to another world and who stared at us as unbelievingly as we stared at them. Pretty well every tribe in Ladakh must have been represented in Leh during our visit, not to mention visitors proudly striding along the main street whose origin we could not even guess; people from Kafiristan in Pakistan, from the Bhamian valley in Afghanistan, from Bhutan or even from "old" Tibet now occupied by China.

In the Himalayas there are no frontiers, only claims. No attempt is made to delineate exactly what belongs to whom, and any sort of control of conflicting demands would be unrealistic anyway, as these mountain peoples take advantage of the confused political situation to establish their own ways of communication virtually without let or hindrance.

In the park at Hemis we came upon a group of tall, fair-skinned people wearing small cloth caps decorated with fresh flowers and chains studded with cowry-shells hanging down over their ears. Nobody knows where these people came from: the only thing that was beyond dispute was that they were Buddhists, a minority from somewhere in the west, perhaps in the Hunza country, living under Moslem rule and now enjoying a stay in Ladakh during the festival after a journey of hundreds of kilometres over passes that can only be negotiated along caravan tracks. There they sat, under the artificially watered poplar trees, staring fixedly at the camera. While I was photographing them I happened to notice a remarkable rectangular brick building without doors or windows. Obviously there must be a courtyard inside, but I should need a ladder to make sure. What secret were those walls hiding? Was it a tomb or some sort of holy place? Or was it haunted? I duly climbed up to the top and looked over the wall. Inside were piles of tree-trunks, neatly stacked and unusually thick, much thicker than the trees in Ladakh are nowadays. But why were they so carefully hidden away, unused and slowly rotting? Purely out of respect: some decades previously Hemis monastcry had been enlarged and these giant trees had had to be cut down. Wood is expensive in Ladakh, yet these trees must have been several generations old to grow to such a size. The monks could not bring themselves to use them for fuel or processing, so they cut the trunks into manageable lengths, stacked them up, and built walls round them to form a sort of sanctuary where they could rest in peace.

Despite the rigours of daily life and the strict demands of their religion, the Landakhis are very keen on sport and practise so many different branches of it that an Englishmen named Edair was able to gather sufficient material for a whole book (long out of print) entitled: "Sport in Ladak". According to a Ladakhi proverb, "work without play is as tasteless as a meal without salt". So the Ladakhis took to polo, introduced by Dards from Gilgit, with such enthusiasm that it became their national sport. In former times this "hockey on horseback" used to be played in the main street of Leh, but so many shops were shattered that a proper polo ground was marked out outside the town and thoroughly watered before each game. In Ladakh, polo is the poor man's chief recreation. Most people own a horse or a pony, and the polo sticks are cut from trees and look more like hockey-sticks. There are no books of rules, and if only ten players are available, the game is five a side: if 24 players turn up, they are divided into two teams of twelve. The British regular officer A. B. Paterson, a first-class player in his day, after watching a game in Ladakh gave the following not very enthusiastic account of it: "The game is very rough and ready, and though the players have little idea of how it should be played, they keep up a terrific pace. They wear dirty coats, and their mountain ponies are tough and tremendously strong, their long tails and manes swirling in the wind. When the team from Gibang really got going, the street had to be cleared, and soon the game became so fast and furious that just after half-time a spectator had to be carted off with a broken leg, though he had only been watching".

Almost as widespread as polo is archery, its popularity stretching from Ladakh to Bhutan and on into Mongolia. Most competitions are held in the spring, just befor sowing begins. Only in Leh is the great competition held during three days in June, depending on the weather. The target, made of white clay and about the size of a dish, is suspended above a small tower about 1–2 metres high. Each competitor has to pay an entry fee and is allowed three shots. His friends encourage him with loud cries of "shok, shok, shok, shok", while his opponents try to put him off with shouts of "kior, kior, kior, kior" (miss it).

Ladakh's most remarkable sports-ground is on an expanse of stones due south of Leh at an altitude of 3700 metres above sea-level: it is the second highest golf-club in the world and boasts five members. It was laid out with the help of an Indian army bulldozer, the sand being made to serve as greens by lavish applications of oil. On page 179 of a guide to Ladakh by Rolf Schettler one can read that "by early in 1975 some of the leading players from Europe's jet-set were playing golf in Leh". I am afraid I have to correct him on this point: the players were neither aces nor members of the European jet-set: they consisted of the Indian District Commissioner of Ladakh, my travelling-companion Axel Thorer of Munich, a friend from Hamburg, and myself.

Over a century ago Hermann von Schlagint-weit-Sakülünski opined that "on the whole the Ladakhis were among the sturdiest and hardest-working people in the whole of Tibet", but at the same time he listed a number of complaints, notably disorders of the stomach and bowels, that brought about a dangerous level of constipation. He eventually found that

---

→

A nomad visiting Leh market.

Page 50–51
A 19-year-old girl with her younger sister.

Page 52–53
Women wearing the velvet hats, and on their backs the sheepskins or goatskins, that are typical of Ladakh.

54

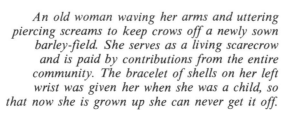

An old woman waving her arms and uttering piercing screams to keep crows off a newly sown barley-field. She serves as a living scarecrow and is paid by contributions from the entire community. The bracelet of shells on her left wrist was given her when she was a child, so that now she is grown up she can never get it off.

Shepherds, beggars, monks, peasants, traders – on all of them the climate and their way of life have left their mark. Their reactions to the camera range from distrust to curiosity, the most friendly character being the one in the bottom right-hand corner: the protruding tongue is a traditional gesture of welcome among Tibetans.

←

Page 56
Dressed in rags, but smiling, for he is sure that he will receive help from the gods to whom he prays with his copper prayer-wheel.

Page 57
Indifferent to the camera's inquisitive eye, a mother fondly cuddles her baby. The elaborate head-dress, studded with turquoise and precious metals, is handed down from one generation to another.

A variety of Ladakh types: a shepherd fastening prayer-banners at the summit of a pass; a visitor from Hunza wearing a hat decked with flowers; caravan leaders giving the camera surly looks; and a man turning to look at a married woman, and with good reason, for Tibetan women, despite their somewhat brusque manner, have an attraction that is all their own.

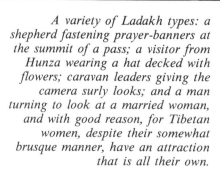

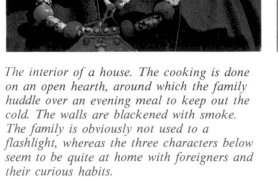

The interior of a house. The cooking is done on an open hearth, around which the family huddle over an evening meal to keep out the cold. The walls are blackened with smoke. The family is obviously not used to a flashlight, whereas the three characters below seem to be quite at home with foreigners and their curious habits.

Among the inmates of the camp for Tibetan refugees near Leh are a married couple who operate a smithy. Among their belongings are relics of earlier expeditions – skiing-glasses, a cloth-hat, and a petrol-can. The young girl playing the flute is wearing a silk "Lhasa" dress, and the old lady on the right is holding her prayer-wheel aloft in homage.

61

The lower the standard of living, the closer the peasants draw to their animals. In a field at Sangskar, the woman drags the family's yaks along by their nose-rings while the man steers the plough.

When the animals are driven up to their high summer pastures, their young, in this case a calf and a terrier, are transported in saddle-bags, but when they are grown up they have to walk, except when their masters carry them across icy torrents.

Two contrasting
young faces from the
land behind the
Himalayas. Above, a
shepherd's son with
matted hair and a
distinctly
unprepossessing
expression: below, a
Leh trader's
daughter, better
groomed and not
quite so frightened.
Both are five years
old.

they were caused by the Ladakhi's indigestible diet and the constant loss of body-fluids. On the other hand many travellers, including myself, have stressed again and again the Ladakhis' extraordinary impassivity and their imperviousness to cold. Living at from three to five thousand metres above sea-level they suffer less from cold than from heat, which for them begins at temperatures at which we still feel distinctly chilly. As Schlaginweit puts it: "Although we were still 3886 metres up, and the noonday temperature never rose much above 15° C, the porters were complaining of being exhausted by the heat: the trouble was due mainly to dark clothing and inadequate headgear".

Nevertheless, Ladakhis often live to extreme old age. Alexander Cunningham, a somewhat pedantic statistician, came across a number of centenarians, including a Sakte nun aged 110. And Schlaginweit encountered at Hemis monastery a monk named Dundup who had reached the age of 103.

From Cunningham's statistics, as well as from the 1971 census, it seems that the population of Ladakh has remained almost steady for the last 120 years, due first to the relatively high proportion of unmarried persons, mainly monks and nuns, and secondly to two local factors: short-term marriages, and more particularly, polyandry.

There are a number of good reasons for this practice. In the first place, scratching a bare living out of infertile soil is a laborious business. For large families, the only alternative to starvation is dispersal or emigration. On the other hand family life is the basis of Ladakh's social order. Secondly, polyandry originated at a time when the Ladakhis were still nomads, and groups of males are more mobile than groups of women encumbered by children. The people of Ladakh maintain that polyandry preserves properties intact, because if a property had to be divided up among a number of sons, the portions would be too small to provide each son with a livelihood. So how does polyandry still function, even though it is no longer as popular as it used to be, because nowadays families can live on goods imported by road from Srinagar?

The wife of the eldest son is also automatically the wife of one of her brothers-in-law. The third son usually enters a monastery, and the fourth (if there is one) becomes a "magpa", a "serving husband" in a family where all the children are female. He has to work and beget children: he can be the property of several sisters simultaneously and is a component of a matriarchy. Yet there are said to be still some families, especially in Lower Ladakh, where one woman is married to up to five brothers but is not, as in some other similar communities, the head of the family. This title is reserved for the eldest brother and "Number One" husband. The status of the other brothers is defined in the colloquial language of Landakh, the word for "uncle" also meaning "little father".

It is forbidden to marry parents' relatives: members of the same family may only inter-marry at intervals of 3 or 4 generations.

Divorce and remarriage are impossible. Up till a few years ago it was the custom to present an unwanted husband with an animal and then turn him out. Heber reports on this unwritten law: "When the husband is asked to leave, he has a right to a pony. If it is the wife who is not wanted, she can claim a cow". One essential condition was that the animal must still be strong enough "to make a circuit of the dunghill unassisted".

Any man or woman, in theory at any rate, may marry twice, especially if, for instance, the woman is barren; and in such cases the husband is requested to take in the wife's place her younger sister without undue ceremony. But the first wife remains the "Number One", even if her younger sister bears children.

To my mind these arrangements are very sensible, though they are no longer applicable to the present-day social structure of India. And they have achieved the desired effects of keeping the Ladakhis working on their land, of preventing over-population, and of evolving a social structure acceptable to nomads, shepherds, peasants, monks and traders alike. Yet even here the construction of road-links with the outside world and the emergence of the age of tourism have wrought changes. The short-term marriages which often lasted only one day and were favoured only by Moslems in the Kargil area are virtually a thing of the past, and even the old traditional burial rites are now confined to one or two remote villages.

Walking through Leh in a north-westerly direction one eventually comes upon the cemetery which today is the last resting-place of the first foreign tourists who were the victims of mischance or their own carelessness. Among its most prominent features is a brick incinerator with a lofty perpendicular chimney. So Leh has a crematorium. After being borne through the city in a curtained rickshaw the corpses (unseen by the congregation) slide down a chute into the ovens, accompanied by offerings for the dead.

In former times, when "the silver cord was loosed or the golden bowl was broken" (Ecclesiastes) the Lama used to be summoned to read from the scriptures and pronounce exorcism. The closest relative had to break the corpse's neck to release the soul, and then the body was rolled up into a ball and placed upon a bier in the family chapel. The right to be cremated was reserved to Lamas and local dignitaries. After lying in the family chapel the body was transported to the desert, dismembered and thrown to the vultures. Another curious custom in former times was that people who had died of an infectious disease were buried for a year before being cremated. As for babies, they were disposed of by being walled up in one of the walls of the living-room.

The months when the sun is lower in the sky and winter looms are the heyday of Ladakh's traders; and the visitor can appreciate the Ladakhis' talent for making the most complicated calculations sith the most simple objects and parts of their bodies. Take their "rosaries" for instance: the beads on the right-hand side are the multiplication units, while those on the left-hand side are the units awaiting multiplication. Hands are ideal calculating machines: a finger has three joints, so not counting the thumbs, which are used as indicators, one can count up to 24 on one's two hands. A combination of finger joints and "rosary" beads can produce almost infinite numbers.

Another rather theatrical method of bargaining is used in horse-trading, which is carried on in public, though how much the buyer is prepared to pay or how much the seller is asking must be kept secret, otherwise they would both lose face. So the buyer places two fingers under the long wide sleeves of the buyer's coat, whereupon the latter protests and puts five fingers under the seller's sleeves. Then the gap between the two prices is gradually narrowed until eventually the buyer first puts two fingers under the seller's sleeve and then three. In other words, the buyer offered 200 rupees for the horse, the seller asked 250, and the horse was eventually sold for 230. Which brings us to the dumb friends that play such a vital part in Ladakhi life, even living on the ground floor of the house (or in a tent) in winter. The yak is as indispensable to its master as he to it.

For a long time nobody seemed to know what these shaggy animals with their long branching horns really were. In his book "Fifty years among Tibetans" (1921) G. Heyde wrote: "Yaks are not found at altitudes below 3000 metres above sea-level. The yak is a curious mixture of goat, horse and ox and is the Tibetans' greatest asset. Its bushy, silvery-white tail and its long black silken hair reaching almost to the ground are used for weaving clothes and black tents". But that is by no means all the yak provides. It gives milk, its dung is used as building material, its flesh is edible, and its horns can be made into drinking vessels. As a beast of burden the yak can keep a foothold on even the steepest path; it can be ridden; and its bones find their way into glue-boilers. In short, they are really astonishing animals: not only can they carry loads of up to 100 kilograms, but if there is no water they are quite happy munching snow. They are led by reins attached to a nose-ring (page 62). Unlike horses, which are constantly short of breath at high altitudes, they conserve their breath by limiting their exertions to movements that require little oxygen.

Ladakh is rich in all kinds of animals, from antelopes and wolves to snow-leopards and the mighty Ovis Ammon, a wild sheep with horns 1.3 metres long and 45 centimetres in diameter at their base. I was once presented with a medium-sized horn and it is now mounted above my front-door. Though I am not particularly partial to trophies, I could not resist Ovis

Ammon, which is now so scarce as to be virtually threatened with extinction.

The Ladakhis are past-masters of the art of setting traps, especially for snow-leopards and wolves, which are hunted down relentlessly and with the utmost cruelty because they constitute a menace to the Ladakhis' most precious possession, their flocks. A sheep is tied up in a bottle-necked pit, and after pouncing on it the leopard is stoned to death, primarily to avoid damage to its valuable skin. Wolves are trapped in a most ingenious and elaborate contraption: a heavy boulder is balanced on poles to which fresh meat is attached. The wolf goes for the meat, knocks against the poles, dislodges the boulder and is crushed by it.

At first sight many of the practices of these people behind the Himalayas may seem illogical, but careful thought will usually reveal that "there is method in their madness". For instance, women wear their fur coats what we should call inside out (pages 52 + 53), whereas in Europe we do exactly the opposite because we are less concerned with keeping warm than with showing off the fur. The Ladakhis carry their furs on their backs, slung over their shoulders from a cord, using the leather to sit on and the fur to keep themselves warm. What seems to us an even more bizarre practice is that when they are short of water they pray to the sun, and with good reason, for it is the spring sun that melts the snow and starts the rivulets flowing down the slopes again. In other words, it is the sun that irrigates Ladakh.

The Ladakhis have devised a highly ingenious method of appeasing the gods and demons with a scapegoat whenever a calamity overtakes an entire community. As it frequently proves impossible to identify the real scapegoat, an innocent victim is selected and banished for one year before being relieved by another equally innocent inhabitant.

Particular care is taken to safeguard children from evil spirits. A little girl, for instance, is given one of the yellow caps worn by nuns although nobody has the slightest intention of actually confining her in a monastery (page 138, above). But the evil spirit, unaware that he is being tricked, leaves the girl severely alone.

Sometimes a baby is colled "Drogma" even though the family are not "drogpas" (nomads) and the baby is a boy, not a girl. The parents put their faith in an old belief that evil spirits are more likely to infest male children, but avoid descendants of the immigrants from Gilgit who first came to Ladakh as Moslems. While playing golf early one morning the Deputy Commissioner (the senior official in Ladakh) had a bright idea: in the new theatre above the town the best dancers in the neighbourhood should give a show for the two dozen or so tourists visiting Ladakh. It was to be a long and enchanting programme that would be sure to be enthusiastically acclaimed by the Ladakhis as well as by the tourists. Ladakhi dancers are slow; male dancers never indulge in wild leaps across the stage and hardly ever dance with women. Every movement in a Ladakhi dance has a definite meaning. The dances are miniature dramas that the audience can follow and interpret; which is why every movement is nearly always carefully rehearsed: improvisation is discouraged. The movements symbolise elements of the everyday life of Ladakh: harvest, death, a wedding, the weather, or the conflict between good and evil. During the actual performance, which lasted over three hours, all eyes were on a small, slight woman wearing a mask. Her movements were so graceful, so eloquent that the audience kept clamouring for "encores". She was the only one of the dancers to emanate an aura of sensuality, among the other dancers as well as among the audience. At the end she took off her mask to reveal the face of an old woman, bathed in perspiration, only her movements had been those of a young girl. And as the applause swelled louder and louder the old woman's features remained completely immobile.

Monks and Nuns

When the Swedish explorer Sven Hedin arrived at Lamayuru monastery on 28th July 1906 seven monks were performing a cabalistic dance. Unimpressed, he noted in his diary: "How bored these monks must be in their self-imposed imprisonment! Obviously their sole distraction is showing off their religious fanaticism for the entertainment of casual tourists". On my first visit to Lamayuru I too witnessed a ceremony by which, unlike Sven Hedin, I was immensely impressed.

Entering the monastery by the main gateway one finds oneself in a courtyard open on the valley side, and a few steps further on is the kitchen door. On the left, stairways lead up to closed doors, behind which are cells and rooms reserved for meditation. Past the kitchen the path gradually becomes steeper. Wooden steps painted red eventually lead up to the central building, but from the facade it is difficult to determine its height. I should imagine that it has at least four floors. Monks and lay assistants in wine-red robes were standing around in the courtyard. One or two of them were laughing at the bewildered expressions on the tourists' faces, others were going quietly about their business. Kitchen-boys were carrying dishes of stew from the kitchen to the central building, and every now and then young lads brought the cooks fuel to warm up their copper cooking utensils. From far off came a sort of humming sound, punctuated by shrill trumpet fanfares. It was the noonday hour of meditation, and from the buildings dotting the slopes above the green valley monks could be seen making their way to the main building. The Kenpo (abbot) came up to me, and surprised at being addressed in Tibetan agreed to detail a monk to show us over the monastery. I took a photograph of the Dalai Lama out of my pocket, told the abbot that I had been the Lama's teacher in Lhasa, and presented him with the photograph. Though I had often before witnessed the awe which a photograph of the Dalai Lama inspires among monks, I have never lost my first impression of wonderment. Taking the bottom of the photograph in both hands the abbot gazed at it and repeatedly pressed it against his forehead until

the monks on their way to meditation stopped to ask what was going on. The abbot duly passed the photograph round, and each monk reacted in exactly the same way as the abbot. The Dalai Lama's powers, the divinity which is apparent even in his photograph, are believed to be transmitted to any monk who applies the photograph to his forehead. This is far from the kind of servility that characterises kissing the Pope's ring or the tips of his shoes: this is real veneration coupled with the desire to be imbued with the divinity of the Dalai Lama. Thanks to the photograph, the whole of Lamayuru monastery was placed at my disposal. In the great refectory the monks were already assembled for the day's third period of meditation (the first period is at 3 a. m.). It was a very large room with an extensive view of the valley below, but despite the brilliant sunshine the refectory was distinctly chilly. Twenty monks were sitting facing each other on two long rows of low benches, and in the background was a kind of altar hidden by thangkas of various sizes and symbolic designs. It was these thangkas that involved us in the only embarrassing incident during my visit. One of my travelling companions knocked his head against a thangka and was immediately glared at by the prayer-leader. A monastery-policeman was summoned and unceremoniously removed the culprit from the refectory. The prayer-leader requested me gently but firmly to take steps to ensure that the furnishings of the refectory were not profaned by my companions. The seating arrangements at prayer and meditation are governed by strict regulations, which are rigidly enforced by the monastery-police. In closest procimity to the prayer-leader (the Gelong, page 73) sit monks in yellow cloaks (page 78, below) denoting that they have passed a number of examinations, and by the entrance sit monks with musical instruments. Between them are the remaining monks and, in the third row, half hidden by pillars and immediately under the windows, sit the novices.

It frequently takes over 20 years' study to become a Gelong. He has to know all the 253 rules governing the ritual and be prepared to submit to the most testing examinations in logic. He ranks second only to the abbot who greeted us on arrival. These two in turn owe allegiance to the Rinpoche. Rinpoches are "begotten, not made", they are re-incarnations of semi-divine beings. A re-incarnation can be a 3 months old baby or a 14 year old boy like the Drugpa Rinpoche of Hemis monastery.

The Gelong of Lamayuru sat with his legs crossed before a tiny wooden desk on which lay an open manuscript. Under his yellow cloak he was wearing a red robe; in his right hand he was holding a bronze thunderbolt, in his left a bell (page 73), the former symbolising masculinity and the latter femininity. The bell also gives the signal for the intonation of the various prayers. Throughout the proceedings the Gelong gesticulates with his thin arms and long bony hands like a conjuror or orator – or even a conductor, but his chin and wispy, snow-white beard remain sunk on his chest throughout. Just how important these gesticulations are is shown by the behaviour of the young gong-beater (page 79). For hours on end he sits at his 50 centimetres high gong looking backward over his shoulder and beating it blindfold, so to speak, as he can never take his eyes off the Gelong. Even our powerful lights for the TV cameras failed to disturb his concentration; he just sat there beating his bright yellow gong, which was suspended from an elaborately carved gilt frame, his gaze ever alert for the Gelong's cue. Gongs are only used in ceremonies directly concerned with the veneration of Buddha. Other instruments, such as the oboes resembling trumpets, are used for conjuring up spirits, evil as well as good, which serve as tutelary deities. There are also small double-gongs made of two human skulls: they are used to signal the intervals between the various ceremonies.

During prayer, the Gelong holds in his left hand a silver bowl shaped like a human skull, into which he dips two fingers of his right hand. The bowl contains the Tibetan beer known as chang, which looks like anis diluted with water. The Gelong sprinkles the chang into the air as a symbolic offering for the forthcoming midday meal. The gesture is by no means arbitrary, but obeys strict rules governing the exact positioning of the fingers, and it also has a deeper significance: together with the music and the

hours of intensive prayer it is conducive to the utmost spiritual concentration.

For our accommodation some of the monastery's outlying buildings were opened up and proved to contain some fine frescoes several metres in length. In the library were tomes of Tibetan literature of considerable value, and just under the roof of one of the towers a thangka artist (page 78) had set up a studio. At the personal request of his fellow-monks his work was on traditional lines, based on strict rules that had been observed for hundreds of years. The artist had no hesitation in offering us some of his works.

There are 40 major monasteries in Ladakh, and 60 smaller ones. Every town or village owns one, or vice versa. The chief monasteries, though not necessarily the largest or most beautiful, are Hemis, Nimaun, Skara, Spittuk, Tiktse, Pyang, Stagna, Languchta, Saspol, Ridzong, Chimre, Massu, Sakte, Likir, Sangskar and Lamayuru. The total number of monks and nuns is debatable, as no official figures are available. In their guide to Ladakh the Swiss writers Pierre Jacard and Pierre Vitoz give estimates of 1,600 and 100 respectively, though in his book "Buddhist Kashmir" Professor F. M. Hassnain puts the number of monks at no fewer than 15,000, but reduces the number of nuns to 50.

As already mentioned, there has been no appreciable increase in the population of Ladakh since 1830, so it may well be that the most accurate figures are those given by Alexander Cunningham, but even these are based on guesswork, as he himself admits: "In quoting 12,000 as the number of people professionally engaged in religious practices, I have had to rely on somewhat vague estimates put forward by other people. There are those who estimate the number of monks and nuns at 20,000, but from personal observations I should say that the true figure would be closer to 10 or 12 thousand".

Not only is Ladakh divided into Indian and Chinese territory, but its Buddhists are also divided into "red-caps" and "yellow-caps". These two sects have managed to co-exist in a severely constricted area since the 14th century, just as Protestants and Catholics have in most of Europe. The great monastery at Tiktse, for instance, belongs to the yellow-caps, whereas at Hemis all the monks are red-caps.

A year after my first visit to Ladakh I made an expedition to Sangskar, a high valley in the extreme south of the country. On the way I met an elderly monk who turned out to be the Trimpön of Karcha monastery. To me, he was just a friendly old man, but his monastic brothers went in terror of him because being one of the monastery's senior dignitaries he is entitled to inflict punishment. As a sign of his authority, one of his two companions was waving a long whip attached to a stick. The Trimpön invited me to take part in an open-air service on an expanse of stones, a rite celebrated once a year in honour of the dead and in expectation of a good harvest. Dozens of monks were assembled, their brilliant robes contrasting vividly with the grey of the stones (pages 74 + 75). The altar consisted of small stones, beside which the Trimpön seated himself. A little further down the slope lay helpers had erected a conical tent. A copper pan was temporarily implanted in the stony ground, and young monks fetched water in bulbous copper vessels like enormous tea-pots (pages 86 + 82 and cover). One lay helper attended to the fire, and every now and then another one lifted the wooden lid off the copper pan, which must have been over one metre in diameter. The cook concocted thick brown butter-tea which was later diluted and handed round to the assembled monks. More and more monks kept arriving, each prostrating themselves before the Trimpön. Some were alone, others came in groups, and within an hour the company numbered some 80 monks, seated on narrow strips of carpet in rows of three at the feet of the Trimpön. The seating arrangements were strictly in accordance with priority and age, the elders sitting closest to the altar. The photograph on page 77 (below) shows the Trimpön in the full glare of the noonday sun, as can be seen from his heavily wrinkled face under his yellow cap. In front of him is a painted table of a type that is very popular in Tibet: it is 40 to 50 centimetres high and can be folded to serve as a sort of tray. On it are the two sacred symbols, the thunderbolt and the bell.

The service began, but still monks came straggling up the slope, most of them elderly and walking with the aid of a stick. The service was constantly interrupted by somebody or something. In the niche housing the altar a butter-lamp was lit, illuminating a pile of piously decorated offerings. Presently a horse appeared upon the scene: its owner had driven it up here from the village below as a present from the peasants in gratitude for the monks' prayers. On the horse's back was a substantial load of barley.

I watched two monks cooking their meal. They had left some tea in the wooden "cups", and this they proceeded to mix with barley, packing the mixture into small cloth bags carried underneath their cloaks. With great care and consummate skill they kneaded a brew of tea and barley, first with one finger, then with two, and finally with the whole of their hands.

Anyone who has ever attended such an outdoor service of prayer will never forget the experience, be it in the sombre refectory of Lamayuru monastery or on this sun-drenched stony slope in Sangskar. Particularly impressive, for all their austere monotony, are the litanies, during which the sacred words "Om mani padme hum" are chanted over and over again. The generally accepted translation given by any good dictionary is "O jewel in the lotus-flower", "Om" stands for the trinity of speech, body and soul, though another version prefers Buddha, teaching, and community. "Mani" are the jewels that God holds in his right hand like the beads of a rosary: they symbolise the road to salvation. "Padme" is the lotus-flower, the symbol of purity, that God holds in his left hand. Finally, "hum" means "bless me". So a literal translation of these sacred words would be "Thou God who holdest in thy right hand the rosary of jewels, and in thy left hand the lotus-flower, the symbol of purity, grant me Thy blessing in spirit, body and soul". The important word is "om", which is intoned in a long, low note and sounds like "omm". Frequently the monks hold the note till they run out of breath. Anyone who has tried this at home will appreciate the impact of this "melody" in appropriate surroundings.

Such dark low notes, echoing in the clear air,

seem to resound all over Ladakh. At Likir monastery the monks are summoned by the beating of a wooden beam, which produces a strikingly similar sound. At Ridzong, a monastery near Khalatse, a gong made of stone is used. It consists of a hollowed-out tree-trunk stopped at one end with a large stone, the sound being produced by hitting it with another stone about the size of a fist.

In my view, a thorough knowledge of the religion practised by thousands of monks and tens of thousands of lay Ladakhis is essential for an understanding of the country they live in. In his book "Heinrich Harrers Impressionen aus Tibet", Martin Brauen devotes 244 pages to Tibetan theology. This is the gist of what he has to say.

"Many books about Tibet maintain that the Tibetan religion is the formative element of the country's life and culture ... yet little or nothing is said about the faith of the lay population. This is a serious error, because this faith comprises many elements of Buddhism. A distinction should be drawn between on the one hand the strictly dogmatic Buddhism, based on the scriptures and secret unwritten traditions, of a small religious minority constantly engaged in abstruse philosophical studies and tirelessly in search of secret spiritual revelations and inner redemption, and on the other hand the religion of the laymen and unlearned monks, who seldom if ever engage in religious studies but are imbued with a profound personal faith. One might well derive the impression that these are two completely independent and self-sufficient forms of religion with nothing whatever in common; but this is by no means the case. On many issues there is hardly any difference between the two: for instance, the laymen frequently turn to eminent theological dignitaries for advice, and their religion displays very many elements of Tibetan theology. One fundamental difference lies in their conflicting attitudes to actions, phenomena and substances. The dominant tenet of orthodox theology is the vanity of all existence, whereas the religion of the laymen is based on a totally different concept which can best be described as "animistic". The concept of "vanity" was not an original or essential feature of Buddhism. Like

any other religion, Buddhism has undergone substantial modifications during which new aspirations have been envisaged, or articles of belief that were originally deemed of minor importance have gradually been elevated to the status of essential dogma. Buddhism holds that the essence of any object is empty and without substance; or to put it less obscurely, whereas all objects around us may outwardly appear to possess a semblance of content, of individuality and substance, in reality they are merely inflated figments of the imagination, insubstantial and empty. And since all things are essentially empty, it follows that there can be no difference between object and subject, between re-incarnation and Nirvana, between a Buddha and a "worldling". As all things are fundamentally empty, it follows that all things are equal and identical with "Buddhahood". Certain beings, the enlightened ones (Buddhas), are aware of this all-pervading unity, whereas the "worldling" believes in the absolute individuality of his being; and this is the great difference between a Buddha and an unenlightened "worldling". It is for the Buddhist to overcome this unenlightenment and to recognise and experience the all-pervading unity of all things. The religion of the Tibetan layman comprises many non-Buddhist elements. In accordance with the designation "animistic", it views the cosmos as an orderly system of latent forces which, once dispersed, influence each other in accordance with a definitely ordained purpose. These forces are not necessarily attached to a visible object but can emanate from invisible

---

→

A prayer-leader at Lamayuru Monastery spraying Tibetan beer from a silver replica of a human skull. In his right hand is the thunderbolt, the symbol of masculinity.

Pages 74/75
A religious ceremony amid boulders and rubble in Sangskar. The monks with yellow caps are from Karcha Monastery, the head of which is the Dalai Lama's younger brother. They are invoking Heaven's blessing on the fields and giving thanks for the good harvest.

Monks of all ages, from venerable greybeards to young novices with shaven heads.
Right: two inmates of a monastery mixing barley flour with a blend of tea and butter in tiny bowls.
Below: the prayer-leader of Karcha Monastery seated behind a painted folding table at the start of a religious ceremony.

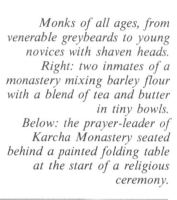

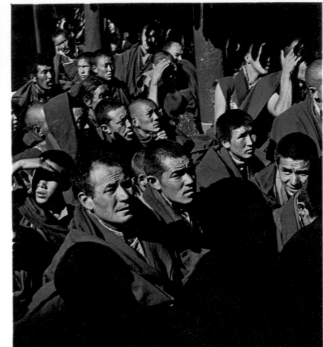

Lamayuru Monastery: a Thangka painter offers his latest work for sale. A shawm player is puffing out his cheeks during meditation. A group of monks in the courtyard waiting for a photograph of the Dalai Lama that they have been promised by the author. Seated on thick cushions the monks are so absorbed in prayer that they hardly notice intruders.

Throughout the ceremony, which can last for hours, this young novice at Lamayuru Monastery never once looks at his gong, but has to beat it without taking his eye off the prayer-leader, who gives him his cue by a particular movement of the fingers.

Page 80 →
The largest prayer-wheel in Ladakh is in Hemis Monastery. Even two strong men can only just move it. The gong contains millions of prayer-banners of up to one metre in length. Each turn of the wheel sets off the bell in the top right-hand corner.

beings or things, even from gods and spirits. Once activated, they remain operative until confronted by a stronger force. The religion of the people attempts to materialise these stronger forces by magic practices and to bring this system, in which everything is influenced by something else, under control, using magic as a kind of knowledge that helps to subudue Nature. The characteristic feature of this view of life is the lack of a supra-natural force which alone and absolutely exercises control over the destiny of the entire cosmos. Instead, it envisages an innumerable array of intricately intertwined forces exerting mutual influences." Such is the gist of Martin Brauen's book, which illustrates the discrepancies between village and monastery, between street and cell.

In Lhasa, most people were afraid of being photographed, believing that whoever got hold of the photograph could, by putting it in his shoe and walking on it, or by consulting a magician, bewitch the person in the photograph. It was generally believed that anyone owning a photograph of someone had magic powers over him. This was just one of many popular beliefs in Tibet, and I was reminded of Lhasa when near Hemis monastery a woman hurried past me holding her yellow cap over her face as a protection against my camera (page 82). From her cropped hair I identified her as a nun. Later she became more approachable and even allowed me to photograph her in front of her cell.

The English traveller Heber, who spent many years in Ladakh, attributed the existence of nuns to the fact that even families who had produced only daughters were anxious to put one of them into a monastery, to dedicate her to God. Most nuns either stay at home or choose cells, like the "eyrie" above Hemis monastery, where they can live alone like hermits; but as at Lamayuru, there are also small convents exclusively for women.

Nuns do not take part in rituals, do not study the scriptures, and are more concerned with physical activities than with spiritual aspirations. Although nuns are not spiritually ordained they are capable (or are believed to be capable, which is even more important) of undergoing remarkable experiences. I was told the following story by a Tibetan monk.

"In the Kongpo district there lived a nun who was periodically possessed by a god. But before being possessed, she had to have a thorough wash, put on a seer's garment representing that of the god by whom she was to be possessed, place a Buddha's crown on her head, and then sit down. Prayers were said and offerings of tea brought in. The nun grew more and more agitated and red in the face; she began to tremble and scream until her features were completely transformed: all of a sudden she looked young and beautiful and quite calm, and even her speech was refined. Now she was ready to answer the questions of the people clustered round her. As the flow of questions began to abate the offerings of tea were reduced until the god departed from the nun's body, whereupon she became quieter and quieter, almost fell asleep, and was suddenly restored to her original appearance".

These three nuns with short
hair and yellow caps only
consent to be photographed
provided they can be sure that
the photographs and
consequently they themselves
will not be bewitched.

83

Rites and Customs

Many customs observed by inhabitants of far-off countries must strike us as bizarre, sometimes even ridiculous. When Maria Heyde, a German pastor's wife who had spent most of her life in Ladakh, was once asked how she managed to endure living among such "peculiar" people, she replied: "You must learn to love them. That's all I have to say. You will find many of their habits extremely strange, and the only thing that will help you is love". Personally I should choose a slightly different word, namely understanding; the kind of understanding that springs from a genuine interest in strange countries and peoples, and from a respect for other peoples' way of life.

Ladakhis wear their best clothes underneath, using their oldest garments as an outer protective covering, but on ceremonial occasions they dress in the reverse order. Hats are not taken off indoors, and like the Tibetans the Ladakhis greet each other by putting their tongues out. Their gardens are on the roofs of their houses and even in the coldest weather they sleep out of doors, naked, and use their clothes as bedclothes.

"To understand this country", wrote the English traveller A. Reeve Heber, "one must constantly bear in mind that it is we who are the intruders and purveyors of strange ideas and habits".

In Sangskar I once saw huts built entirely of yak dung. In summer, when the yaks are up in the high pastures, their dung is collected and used to build huts with sloping walls like European gables. When winter comes these huts are dismantled and taken down to the valleys for fuel.

Designing homes is one of Ladakh's most widespread activities. The most ingenious tricks are resorted to in order to achieve the maximum comfort in a minimum of congenial climate. As a general rule houses are built only on land that cannot be used for any other purpose. Sometimes a house clings to such steep slopes or even rockfaces that they serve as walls. On the roof there is not only a garden but also a small grazing area where the smaller animals can breathe some fresh air in winter.

Balconies are orientated to get the maximum benefit of every possible ray of sunshine, so that as much work as possible can be done in the open air. As well as a large sunny room just under the roof most houses have a second living-room with a big window taking up almost the whole of one wall. The "stove" is made of a special kind of black clay which is extracted from the river-beds and dried out until it is as hard as a brick. The top of the "stove" has a line of holes with high rims into which the cooking utensils are fitted. Every stove has a bellows consisting of a bag made of goat-leather, a tube leading straight into the fire, and two little sticks to regulate the intake of air. It is here that the Ladakhis make their tea, which they drink in vast quantities. The best tea, black in colour, comes from China and is still available at Leh market even though the frontier is closed. It is brewed for hours and then blended with a savoury mixture of butter, soda, salt, and often milk. The Ladakhis attach great importance to the butter smelling good and never having been melted. The final concoction is more like a soup than a drink.

Almost every Ladakhi is good at spinning wool, weaving and dyeing. "After cooking", writes Heber, "spinning is the commonest indoor activity." And with good reason, because most of the valuable wool of which Kashmir shawls are made comes from Ladakh.

The best material, say the Ladakhis, comes from "the great plain to the north" which stretches from near Leh to the Chinese frontier. "Lena", as it is called, is as soft as silk and is cut from the undercoat of wool that sheep grow next to their skins to keep the cold out in winter. Actually however there is an even better material that fetches astronomical prices in Delhi, Bombay or Calcutta. It comes from the neck and breast hair of the Tibetan antelope, and twenty to thirty animals yield no more than about 3½ pounds of it.

There is a story current in Leh about the Mogul Emperor Mizar Hedar, the grandfather of the celebrated Akbar, who travelled to Ladakh to visit the King. The King asked him to conquer the country of Purig for him, a task the Emperor duly accomplished with a force of 500 men, but then claimed the country for himself and annexed it. Nevertheless the King of Ladakh sent his treacherous "friend" some samples of material woven from "Lena", and the Emperor was so delighted with them that he started to trade it and is said to have been the first to order these shawls. Later, two Persian traders appeared upon the scene and took some samples of "Lena" back to Persia. A year later they turned up again and bought some more "Lena". From Persia it found its way to Alexandria and from there across the Mediterranean to Genoa and Venice. Eventually Kashmir wool became a "best-seller" all over the world, but how many people realise that the sheep which yield this wool come from Ladakh?

The roof is the domain of the women of the household, and there they sit behind low walls usually built of dried bundles of lucerne and look down through slits in the walls on the comings and goings in the main street. In Kargil they are permitted to join the men in smoking their hookahs: the mouthpiece is held in the fist, the smoke passes through the hollow of the hand, and the mouth is applied to the semi-circle formed by thumb and forefinger. Old-time travellers in Ladakh used to tell of a now virtually obsolete practice of smoking tobacco without a pipe. Tobacco was plugged into a hole in the ground and set alight, and the smoker bent down, or lay on the ground, and inhaled the smoke through a tube.

As mentioned above, the Ladakhis' treatment of their clothes seems to us rather curious. The extra-long sleeves serve as rough and ready handkerchiefs: shirts, trousers and coats are never washed. But if someone is unexpectedly obliged to dress up for some ceremonial occasion such as receiving the blessing of the head Lama, he can be sure of being able to borrow the necessary garments.

From earliest times the monasteries have been at pains to preserve traditional methods of healing. There is therefore no shortage of "doctors" in Ladakh, though the treatments they administer sound positively terrifying and often have exceedingly disagreeable consequences. Their medical knowledge is derived from the commentaries on Tibetan Sacred Scriptures, amounting to 108 volumes. Doctors can be identi-

fied by the large cloth bags they carry over their shoulders. In these bags are the tools of their trade, the pills and elixirs concocted from wild herbs in spring and summer. Nowadays of course doctors frequently patronise the bazaars for their medicines, and in recent years hospitals have been built at Leh and Kargil, but for treatment in the home the medicine-man is still the only answer.

Most elderly Ladakhis suffer from inflammation of the knees. The doctor examines the knee, has a look at the patient's tongue and feels his pulse, because the pulse is regarded as the key to an accurate diagnosis, no matter whether it is the heart, stomach, lungs, liver, kidneys or spleen that are affected. In due course the doctor pronounces his verdict: the knee must be cauterised with a red-hot iron, a classic example of eliminating a pain by inflicting a more agonising one somewhere else. A pill is prescribed, to be taken with lukewarm water only. As for diet, the meat of white sheep is wholesome, but not that of black sheep. If the patient starts to run a temperature he must on no account be allowed to fall asleep, otherwise he will surely die. Whenever possible he should be dragged to his feet and kept moving. Among less drastic treatments, some of which are not unknown in Europe, are leeches and blood-letting. In the chapter entitled "Spirits and Demons" I shall describe what happens when a Ladakhi asks a soothsayer to draw up a horoscope, but these soothsayers are such an established feature of life in Ladakh that a word or two about them at this point may not be out of place.

Even when making the pilgrimage to the great festival at Hemis monastery a Ladakhi wants to make quite sure that nothing can happen to him. So he consults a soothsayer and is told that Thursday would be a good day to start the journey, only unfortunately there is a slight snag about Thursday: the pilgrim will arrive at Hemis all right but he will be robbed on the

Pages 86/87 →

Lay assistants at Karcha Monastery preparing a blend of tea and butter in the open air. The tent in the background is where the cooking is done.

way. What is to be done? Pretend to start on Wednesday, take seven steps in the direction of Hemis, then turn back, and make a second start on Thursday: this time everything will be all right.

Similar tricks are resorted to in order to abridge readings from the scriptures. If one Lama is invited to a house, he will have to read out ten times as many passages as ten Lamas. So it is better to invite ten Lamas at once: they declaim the obligatory passages simultaneously so that not a single word can be understood. But that doesn't matter: the point is that the passages have been duly read out.

The caste system, as observed in India, is unknown in Ladakh, but there are social grades that in the case of artists and craftsmen are determined by their ethnic origin. "Mön", for instance, (see the chapter "Men and Beasts"), who have for centuries provided Ladakh with musicians, are on the same social level as joiners. Their instrument is a sort of drum in the shape of a bowl, and the sound it produces is remarkably like the sound of the Ladakhi word for them, "dammadam". Another favourite instrument is a sort of oboe or shawn, 60 centimetres long and made of wood and silver. Its tone is very soft and astonishingly flexible. Every village has its story-tellers, who accompany their narrations on home-made stringed instruments and have perfected the art of interrupting their lurid tales with a discordant tune just when their audience is awaiting the climax with breathless excitement. Hundreds of legends and fairy-tales circulate in Ladakh (one of them is quoted in the chapter "Roads and bridges"). Many of them bear a close resemblance to our European stories about good kings, abominable step-mothers, and beneficent spirits. The same applies to proverbs, the only difference being that Ladakhi ones are couched in more flowery language: "A meal without salt is like work without play", or "Parents are their children's judges".

The Ladakh year lasts 360 days, at any rate as far as religon is concerned. It is therefore extremely difficult to determine a person's real age. The Ladakhis solve this problem by adding on extra days or even a whole month, recording his age not in decades but in spans of 12 years. A man born in 1930 for instance is by the year 1978 not 48 but 4 dozen years old. Similarly, a man born in 1931 will say he is 3 dozen and 11 years old.

A Ladakhi's relations with the stars are so close that when they are in danger he does all he can to help them. During an eclipse of the sun for instance he will scream at the top of his voice in order to frighten off "the dragon which is devouring the sun".

The pilgrims who are such a prominent feature of Lhasa are still in evidence in Ladakh, though their number is steadily declining. There are even some particularly devout pilgrims who progress by lying on the ground with their arms outstretched in front of them and then moving their feet up to where the tips of their fingers had been, and so on ... I described one of these pilgrims in my book "Geister und Dämonen": "On our way to the holy mountain (Kailas) we encountered the first of these pilgrims who cover hundreds, thousands even, of kilometres by measuring their length along the ground, and always directly facing the mountain. Particularly devout pilgrims actually measure their breadth along the ground, and it often takes them years to make their laborious way to Kailas or Lhasa. I once met a mendicant who had been propelling himself forward for 15 years. His pigskin coat was old and in tatters, but he had protected his hands with wooden gauntlets. His skin was like very old leather, furrowed and encrusted with the dirt of many years."

In Leh, the pilgrims start at a point about five kilometres west of the town and take three days to proceed by the method described below along the main street, up to the hilltop monastery of Tsomo, round the king's palace, and back to where they started. First they fold their hands over their chests, then kneel down, throw themselves forward on to their arms and stretch them out in front of them. They then scratch a line in the dust with their finger-nails, get up, place the tips of their toes along this line and again project themselves forward on to their arms. They allow themselves rest and refreshment about every two hours; and anyone giving them pap or beer is sure of some religious reward, and so this extremely arduous sort of pilgrimage is not without its brighter side: there is something for everybody.

Like peoples in other continents, the Ladakhis have to observe all sorts of strict customs and tabus concerning births, marriages and deaths. In the villages, a mother is not allowed to work on the land until one month after her confinement. This may seem a very sensible precaution from the point of view of the health of the mother, but the tabu also applies to the father, except that he is allowed to use the paths between the fields. A young mother is also not allowed to cook or even handle a dish or a ladle. Shortly after a birth a (usually male) relative arrives with a bowl of barley-broth which is shared out among all present. On a child's second birthday his or her head is shorn, leaving only a single tuft of hair which is steeped in butter and then bound in a coloured ribbon.

With the possible exception of a funeral, there is no more elaborate ceremony in Ladakh than a wedding. There is a local proverb to the effect that "the father is distressed when he has to find his son a bride", but his distress is nothing compared to what the wretched son has to go through before he is allowed even to touch his bride-to-be. The day of the wedding is often fixed by a soothsayer a year in advance. The parents supply him with the name and age of their child, and the soothsayer then announces the age and perhaps the identity of the future bride or bridegroom, along with a list of the qualifications he or she must possess. Eventually the great day dawns when the father is to have his future daughter-in-law brought to him, and he despatches a friend to fetch her from her home. A conference is then held over beer to work out an agreement or contract. At a second meeting, a list is made of presents for the bride's parents. Money, it is said, is part of Nature, which presented the girl with her very first food in the form of her mother's milk, so the presents usually consist of dried apricots, tea, Tibetan beer, butter, meat, rice and scarves (katas). The third conference takes place two weeks before the day appointed for the wedding and has to decide which member of the family is to provide the food and the utensils for the wedding feast. Usually it is the bride's uncle who provides the cake around which the assembled guests will dance.

The menu for a Ladakhi wedding-feast contains many more liquids than solids. It begins with tea, followed by a mixture of flour, butter, sugar, and dried curds. Then more tea and bread, meat of some kind, and barley-broth diluted with water. The fifth course consists of beer, and the sixth of "Nang-chang", a strong beer of which each guest must drain a full beaker. The seventh course is "Söl-chang", yet another kind of beer, and the feast ends with rice.

But the proceedings are by no means over: the bride has to be fetched by from five to eleven boys, who start off early in the morning dressed in the prescribed silk costumes and tall hats. Bearing with them ample supplies of "chang" they start off for the bride's home, not forgetting the 80-odd duties they have to perform on the way. In front of the bride's home, for example, a stick is buried, and the leader has to find it with his feet. As soon as he has discharged his duties the agreed presents are handed over, but as a precautionary measure both families are armed with clubs which they have no hesitation in making use of if one of the families is deemed not to have fulfilled its obligations. Next, the young men dance across the living-room three times, do justice to a hearty meal and prodigious quantities of beer, leave the house, and dance in the open air round an assortment of meat, bread and beer before what is by now a milling crowd of spectators. Next a young girl appears with burning incense, carrying the bride's wedding-dress for the admiration of all present. In the evening the two families break bread together, the bread being supplied by the bridegroom's uncle, who boasts his authority by wearing a silken band round his middle finger. Then the present-giving and dancing are resumed until the hour deemed by the soothsayer as being most propitious for the actual nuptials, but before they can be concluded a scribe makes an inventory to decide who gets what in the event of a divorce, and a hairdresser goes to work on the bride's hair (at her father's expense). At last the bride appears in a long garment that has been

Ladakhis at work. The woman makes dung-bricks (above) which are dried in the open air and then used for heating. Above: building material for their mud-cottages is another product of the same process. The woman on the right is spinning the thread from which is woven (page 91) a coarse but warm material.

handed down from one generation to another, and wearing a white cap seats herself on a carpet strewn with barley in the shape of a swastika. Her future clothes are strung on a line running right across the room, and beneath them are the pots and pans given her by her parents. A particularly important personage is a monk who confers a new blessing on the house, the former one being deemed to be taken with her by the bride (quite unintentionally of course). He is rewarded with a length of cloth, while the bride's parents are presented with garlands, and the bride's remaining relatives receive small strips of white material.

Now the bride bursts into tears and tells her parents how very, very good they have always been to her. Next, the leader of the boys who originally fetched her from her home conducts her to the house chapel, wich she now enters for the last time: henceforth she will belong to a new family.

And so the guests disperse, the bridegroom's father and uncle giving the bride's parents more garlands and money and thanking them for their presents to the bride before taking their leave. But no matter what hour the soothsayer appointed for the wedding, the bride may only be taken to her new home under cover of darkness, otherwise her parents-in-law have to pay a fine to the nearest monastery (in former times to the king). So once again a monk is required, this time to make sure the bride is not possessed by evil spirits which might "infect" her new home. So the monk takes up a new jug full of dregs of "chang", smashes it, and throws it away.

The bride's introduction to her new home is almost military in its precision: she has to greet her new mother-in-law before being conducted to the living-room, where the bridegroom is seated on the floor. If the bride is marrying several brothers at once (polyandry) they all crowd on to one carpet, but the bride has one to herself. There follow more eating and drinking, and then the bride and bridegroom go to the store-room, where the leader of the boys who first fetched her removes the couple's white headgear, lays them on a silver tray, hands both bride and bridegroom dishes piled with food and asks: "Which of you is the quicker, the bride or the bridegroom?", whereupon each tries to grab the other's dish.

It is in this store-room that the newly-weds will spend the next few days, accepting small cakes and other presents from their relatives. Yet the celebrations are still not over: dancing in and out of doors goes on for days. On one evening there may be 100 to 150 guests, on the next only close relations. And at regular intervals both bride and bridegroom have to pay their respective parents the utmost respect.

For centuries there has been little change in the construction and furnishing of houses in Ladakh. Few tourists have had an opportunity of seeing over a house like the one described from the outside at the beginning of this chapter.

A low front-door opens on to the ground floor, which is in complete darkness and is used for stabling yaks or dzos. One has to grope one's way to a steep flight of stone steps leading to the mezzanine, which consists usually of stone, whereas the upper floors are made of clay bricks. If there is heavy rain, which seldom happens, a wall made of bricks dried in the sun (page 90, above) can simply disintegrate, but curiously enough the owner doesn't let this worry him unduly, he just builds a new wall. The stairs up to the first floor lead straight into the low-ceilinged living-room. The floor is a mixture of clay and pebbles or earth cemented by cow-dung. The walls and ceiling are blackened by smoke (page 60, above), because the hole in the roof and the two window are not enough to ventilate the room from the smoke from an open fire, seeing that the room is used as a kitchen as well as a living-room. The windows are set low down in the walls so that the occupants can see out of them sitting down. Along one of the walls are shelves, partly of wood and partly of bricks, for storing the cooking and eating utensils. Meanwhile the room had become so full of smoke that my eyes started watering, but the Ladakhis seem to be quite impervious to smoke. They huddle round the fire on mats which are used for sitting on in the daytime and for sleeping on at night. In front of them are two tiny tables not much higher than footstools. The living-room is often as large as 6 x 8 metres, but the ceilings are always very low, and I should say that the average living-room is not more than about 1.7 to 2 metres high. The ceilings are made of poplar twigs about as thick as a finger, pared, made into bundles and coated with clay. This somewhat fragile construction is strengthened by wooden supports. Many living-rooms also have a balcony, invariably facing south or west, about 6 metres across and 80 centimetres wide. The doors consist of wooden beams fastened together by nails, strips of metal, or leather. There are also curtains to keep the room warm during the day-time, especially in winter, as the door is only closed at night.

Travellers disagree about the quality and comfort of Ladakh's houses. The German missionary Wilhelm Heyde wrote: "Even the houses are not exactly inviting"; but the British traveller Major Alexander Cunningham thought that "if only these houses had glass windows and proper stoves they would be not uncomfortable. As things are, however, they can only be described as primitive hovels, especially in winter". Since then, most houses have been equipped with glass windows and efficient stoves, which is why I fully agree with the first part of Cunningham's description.

The Ladakhis are semi-nomadic, an existence which is forced upon them by the climate. They spend the winter in their homes down in the valley and the summer in tents or stone huts up in the high pastures. I formed the impression that these people behind the Himalayas had never got used to the idea of settling down in permanent homes. In every village one visits there is a constant coming and going of caravans, nomads, families visiting relatives, and pilgrims. There are still places where travellers can hire horses and guides to ride around in the valleys, if necessary for weeks on end or to visit remote monasteries. As recently as 1976 there was no other way of getting to Sangskar, for instance. Furthermore, this love of travelling also has its religious advantages, as a pilgrimage ensures a better life in the next world, and the monasteries supply pilgrims with food and drink. Seeing that the 1975 Festival at Hemis attracted over 3,000 visitors, and not counting children and old people, a quarter of the entire population must have attended it.

Ladakh's caravan-leaders and nomads are fully conscious of their freedom and independence over an area that once stretched from Srinagar to Lhasa and from Gilgit to Gangtok. They regard with some contempt anyone who has settled down somewhere, and he in turn envies these adventurous spirits who accompanied only by their flocks cross the 5,082 metres Shing-kun Pass to Lahul, or the 5,046 metre Sengi-La Pass to Sangskar, or the daunting 5,563 metre Chalung Pass to Khapaln in Baltistan. These tough nomads ignore politics, frontiers or forbidden zones. True, they are debarred from entering Central Tibet, but as we have seen, tea from Lhasa is still sold in Leh market.

Nevertheless, most Ladakhis abandoned nomadic life and settled down a long, long time ago. There is documentary evidence that ploughs and yokes were introduced in the second century A. D., and 300 years later irrigation was perfected, Terraces were laid out, and dams were constructed against spring spates. Cross-breeding yaks produced dzos, and mules were employed in agriculture and caravans.

These were only the first steps. Next, the Ladakhis turned their attention to trade, but only in the form of barter, as people did not use money in the high valleys. So the peasants gathered wool and bartered it for seeds, cloth, spices and sugar. Later they also traded the salt they extracted from their numerous mountain lakes. The shepherds supplied the lower valleys with butter in exchange for tea, and milk and cream came pouring into the oases of the Indus desert.

The Ladakhis live at an altitude of 2,500–4,000 metres above sea-level. Curiously enough, the higher the land between the Karakorums and the Himalayas, the more fertile it is owing to the moisture from glaciers and snow. Not unnaturally, the Ladakhis seek out these comparatively fertile areas, follow the water-courses, and put the high pastures to good use: shepherds' huts have been seen at an altitude of no less than 5,000 metres.

Unfortunately, this fertility is marred by a shortage of oxygen and it is at the most fertile altitudes that breathing is most difficult. The

Nature is not always bountiful, and the struggle to scratch a bare living is determined by the seasons. What is usually regarded as essentially man's work is often performed by women, and vice versa. The woman on the left is using a goat's horn for weeding, and the man on the right is weaving dung-coloured cloth from coarse yarn. The two women in the middle are stirring butter using leather thongs to rotate a long wooden twirling-stick: the women's movements resemble those of men working a cross-cut saw.

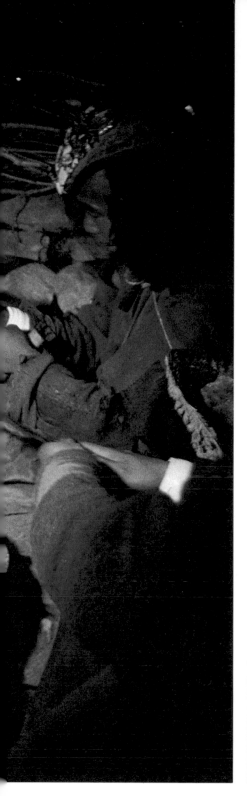

highest altitude at which human beings can exist comfortably is around 4,000 metres above sea-level, as is proved by the fact that for all the unpolluted high valleys, the clear air and the pure water, infant mortality in Ladakh is only negligibly less than in Indonesia or the Philippines, quite apart from the almost total lack of doctors in the European sense of the word. So there were one or two amenities the Ladakhis had to do without. They had goats, sheep, oxen, horses and donkeys as well as a few cats and dogs. But for a long time they had no chickens. Hermann von Schlagintweit wrote: "When we crossed the Himalayas for the second time in May 1856 we took the precaution of stocking up with chickens as presents." Eventually they were introduced by European travellers, and rearing chickens soon became a profitable undertaking, as Buddhism holds that eating eggs is destroying life. Yet nowadays eggs are as normal a feature of the tourist's breakfast as tea without butter.

The ingenuity of the Ladakhis in devising means of living without eating very much is nothing short of astonishing. They have learned by experience physiological facts which Europeans had to wait for scientists to discover in their laboratories. I observed a caravan on the way to Padum, the capital of Sangskar, which was also the place my party was making for. After a long day's trek which had left them over-heated and dehydrated, the men warmed up running water before drinking it. I asked them why they didn't drink it cold and was told that an equal quantity of warm water is healthier and more effective. Hermann von Schlagintweit had made the same observation 120 years previously.

Finally, mention should be made of Ladakh's national drink, the mysterious "butter-tea". Although not in any dictionary, it is on everybody's lips in Ladakh. Maria Heyde, a missionary's wife, copied out a recipe for ten persons: "Take a cupful of tea, boil it in 3 litres of water for 10 minutes, and add a heaped spoonful of natron. Pour the mixture into a churn and add a pound of butter and a spoonful of salt until the mixture attains the consistency of cream". In volume 3 of his book "Reisen in Indien und Hochasien" Hermann von Schlagintweit, who collected statistics of the measurements and temperatures of Himalayans as assiduously as he noted the number of domestic animals they kept, gives a far more accurate recipe for Ladakh's "national drink". "Mix a quantity of tea with half its weight of soda or natron, fairly pure. Next, pour the mixture of tea and soda or natron into a pan of cold water, the number of tea-leaves being somewhat greater than what would be used for strong tea in Europe. Leave the pan on the fire for about 4–6 minutes after the liquid has started to boil and keep stirring. After removing the vessel from the fire pass the contents through a strainer, and pour the liquid into a wooden pot. Stir the tea and add a generous measure of melted butter, about twice the weight of the tea-leaves, as well as some salt. Pour the tea back into the pan, add milk and heat the mixture once more, as during the stirring the tea will have gone very cold. You now have a fairly thick fluid that can be enjoyed at any time of the day, especially at mealtimes. Only during certain religious ceremonies is its consumption forbidden".

The above process is illustrated in the photograph on pages 86 and 87: a lay brother is pouring concentrated butter-tea into a large pan temporarily implanted in the ground, while a lay helper serves diluted tea in a copper jug. It was exceedingly difficult to photograph women engaged in preparing one of the country's staple foods, i. e. butter. They were frightened of a man intruding upon them because the presence of a man, they maintained, would not only turn the butter sour but also diminish the yield. Eventually two women in Sangskar promised to let me watch the process on condition that I didn't tell anyone else. In the meantime however word had gone round that I was a friend of the Dalai Lama's and the women gave in; they must have convinced themselves that a man with such an exalted friend could only increase the yield. Yet there was nothing secret or mysterious about the way they made butter (pages 94 + 95, middle). In a large wooden tub on the ground was a twirling-stick, its other end being attached to the wall. Round this stick the two women had wrapped a broad strip of leather. Standing side by side, each held on to one end of the leather by a wooden handle and rotated the stick extremely vigorously. Such was their concentration that not a single word was spoken, the only sound that escaped their lips was a soft humming. A folk-song perhaps, or a tune they had specially selected for this process? Not at all: they were simply counting from 1 to 1,500, by which time the butter would be set.

That evening one of the women came to our tents and handed me a lovely bowl of warm yak's milk and a slab of butter which was so incredibly dirty that I could hardly bring myself to put it in my tea.

The British doctor A. Reeve Heber entitled the last chapter of his book "The lure of Ladakh" and in it described the irresistible urge to return there again and again. I heartily agree: ever since I first crossed the Potu-La pass in 1974 I have been back every year to revisit the gods and mere mortals behind the Himalayas. Perhaps their charm, of the mortals at any rate, is best illustrated on a very solemn occasion: when Ladakhis sign an agreement they seal it with the words: "and this shall stand until the crows in the air turn white and the glaciers in the mountains turn to water". Could there be a more honourable or enduring promise?

Three Ladakhis from the province of Sangskar irrigating their land. Each family is allocated a ration of water corresponding to its availability and their requirements, and long poles are used to channel it through an ingenious network of conduits.

Leh, Ladakh's Capital

1 50 years ago the place must have looked almost exactly the same as it does today. The population was the same, the green fields lining the River Indus were the same, and even the houses have hardly changed at all. The palace, that looks remarkably like the Potala in Lhasa, still looms menacingly over the town, and the fortress high above the palace was ruined even in those days (pages 106/107). The tiny "penthouse" perched above the main street probably looked as unsafe then as it does now (page 114), and today's visitor to Leh will not be surprised by anything particularly up-to-date. Yet there are one or two minor differences. In those days the palace was occupied by a king, and there were no hideous overhead cables spanning the streets at a dangerously low level. The shelter for the policeman by the bazaar did not exist and there were no cars. Monks departed on pilgrimages to Lhasa every week, and caravans arrived from Central Tibet, which is now a forbidden zone. In short, Leh had not yet been "discovered".

When Hermann von Schlagintweit rode past the great "Stupas" over a hundred years before I did, the sight that met his eyes, if his drawings are to be believed, could have been somewhere in Arcadia, a lovely little town nestling in an environment of gentle hills (page 101). Forty years later Sven Hedin made a drawing of the town fron a totally different aspect, that of a grim bastion surrounded by high mountains (page 101). Both drawings are accurate, only they reflect the eye of the beholder, not the nature of Leh itself.

Today we know Leh inside out. There are town-plans, a Post Office, a number of restaurants, a military airfield, and a power-station that provides electricity for an hour or two every evening: it can be heard and smelt kilometres off. For a lot more information about Leh we owe a debt of gratitude to the Indian Civil Servant J. N. Zutshi. It was he who worked out that Leh numbers 5,519 inhabitants, 1,157 of whom have a house of their own; that only one in three of the population can read and write; that there are more males than females; that half the population have jobs; that in the urban district there are 621 peasants

and 271 industrial workers; that 125 persons earn their livelihood from lorries, at the Post Office, or in warehouses; and that 20 men and one woman work in mines or quarries.

Although it is really only an overgrown village, Leh is marked on any map of Asia. It is the only town in a mountainous wilderness stretching away for hundreds of kilometres to Lhasa and China. Leh has always been a staging-post between the Middle East and Central Asia. So let us see what travellers who visited this royal residence on the River Indus between 1852 and 1974 had to say about it.

The British traveller Alexander Cunningham contents himself with the information that Yak wool can be bought on the market in all sorts of different colours; that the ferry over the River Indus is propelled by inflated tubes made of goat leather; and that deaths amount to no more than 50 a year at the most. In a book over 500 pages long only 12 lines are devoted to the royal palace at Leh: "It is an extensive, handsome building high up above the city. It is 75 metres long and has 7 stories. The outer walls are tremendously thick but get thinner towards the top. The upper stories have wide uncovered balconies facing south, and along the walls are an astonishing number of windows. The beams across the ceiling are supported by carved pillars and covered with boards painted in a number of different patterns. Although the building is somewhat ungainly and massive, its height and its proportions create a distinctly impressive effect".

The next to describe Leh was the German missionary Wilhelm Heyde, who left Kothgur on 26 March 1855 and arrived in Leh early in April. He too failed to generate much enthusiasm for the place. The following description is taken from his biography written by his son: "This town stands in a sandy plain at the intersection of a number of caravan routes. It has a large market-place (bazaar) and is dominated by a fine old royal palace".

In 1869 Hermann von Schlagintweit had more

→

Two views of Leh: the water-colour (above) is by Hermann von Schlagintweit, and the pencil-sketch (below) is by Sven Hedin.

to say about the local houses than about their occupants: "Several houses in the town, perhaps five or seven, have more than one balcony and were altogether superior to most houses in Tibet, but even in these houses the only pretensions to "style" are the symmetrical arrangements of architraves above the balconies, dormer-windows and doors; the wooden galleries running right round the inner courtyards at first-floor level or higher; and one or two wooden ornaments that are clearly of Indo-Buddhist origin".

The English traveller A. Reeve Heber and his wife Kathleen, who visited Leh in 1902, were the first to pay any attention to its inhabitants, and with one or two modifications his description still applies today: "The market is crowded with all sorts of different people. Attractive Jarkandis rub shoulders with slit-eyed Tibetans; a Kulu or his neighbour from Latul do business with a shepherd from Baltistan, Kashmir or one of India's northern provinces. But what business? The Jarkandis from the far north offer brilliantly coloured carpets; snow-leopard, fox, wolf, beech-marten and beaver skins; silk from Khotan, and thick felt mats. The exceedingly arduous journey to Leh takes them over a month, and sometimes the path can only be identified by the skeletons of men and animals lining it. As soon as they have sold their stock the Jakandis move on further south to buy material which they can sell in their own country. They frequently combine business with religion by making the journey in late summer and going on to Bombay, whence they embark upon a pilgrimage to Mecca. They come back next year and return to their native land in the autumn.

Then there are the Tibetans, trying to persuade Baltis to accept cooking butter and dried apricots in return for salt, borax and Lhasa tea.

The nomads from Changtang offer the featherweight wool of their long-haired sheep; the Kashmiris take it with them down to their valleys and use it for making their famous shawls.

A man from the Kulu valley has brought petroleum to Leh market, and occasionally one or two china cups, while a trader from India offers German cloth, brocade for the Ladakhis' elaborate ceremonial dress, underwear, tea, cigarettes, spices and all the 101 commodities a housewife needs to run her house properly.

The best time to visit Leh market is in autumn, when trade is at its most brisk and the traffic grinds to a halt because the wares are laid out all over the road and even pedestrians can hardly pick their way through them, as quite apart from the merchandise people from far and wide block the streets with their yaks, dzos, donkeys, horses and mules."

Four years later Sven Hedin arrived and concentrated primarily on acquiring equipment for his expedition to Central Tibet. "Leh is the last proper town on the road to Tibet, and the last place where we would be able to buy any equipment, so I could not afford to forget anything: if I did, we should have no further chance of replenishment. We spent rupees like water, but I consoled myself with the thought that we should soon be in a county where we wouldn't be able to spend a farthing even if we wanted to. In countries with shops and markets a major expedition eats up money like a vampire sucks blood, but as soon as all links with civilisation are severed, an expedition has to depend on its own resources: if it is unable to fend for itself, it is doomed".

In geographical terms, Leh is an oasis in a lateral valley running from the river Indus, which rises at Kailas, Asia's holy mountain, 500 kilometres distant. The valley is enclosed on three sides by hills, with minor elevations stretching down to the river. Only at noon do the grey, bare rocks take on a brownish tinge. They are entirely devoid of trees, bushes, grass or even moss. Every clod of earth in their crevices has been swept away by water or blown away by wind. Immense sand-dunes stretch down to the river on both sides of the valley, which is why the whole area is known as

---

Pages 102/103

An outdoor school. Assembled on either side of an irrigation canal, the children are taught in three languages: Tibetan, their native language; Hidi, the official language; and Urdu, the language of everyday life.

104

the "Indus desert". In the background, like a backcloth in a theatre, are the high mountains, first gently sloping and almost symmetrically conical, then precipitous and jagged. Even in June and July slopes have a thin covering of snow, which higher up takes the form of glaciers.

A glance at the great granite rock overhanging the town, with a tiny monastery clinging to the rockface, emphasises the abrupt contrast between the green of the oasis and the ochre of this desert. A well-watered field gives way to a dusty road beyond which there is nothing but an endless expanse of sand. It is as if the dividing line between civilisation and wilderness had been cut by a sword.

Approaching the town along the river one experiences an optical illusion. Ahead lies Leh, clear, distinct and imminent; with houses sprawling along the slopes on the right, the great Stupa on the left, the windows, balconies and massive walls of the palace, and above it the monastery and castle brooding over the town. Then comes a bend in the road and all of a sudden Leh is completely lost to view. The seven stories of the building with the "penthouse" precariously balanced on its roof (page 114) are suddenly reduced to two: the view is blocked by the Stupa at the main gate.

The rectangular base of this Stupa is brick-red. On all four sides are carved and brightly coloured likenesses of fabulous beasts, two pouncing to the left and two to the right (the beats on page 133 are snow-leopards). On the saddle of a wild horse is the triple jewel, the Norbu, symbolising religion and bringing wealth and good fortune. From the base, known to Buddhists as the "throne", five steps lead up to a dome-like structure, each step having a special significance of its own. The first is the "holy carpet" on which the Lama seats himself. The next two represent the legs, the last two the arms, and the dome the head of a symbolic body with no apparent posterior. On the head is a cylinder of 13 brick rings representing the 13 ages of Buddhism (an age = 100,000 years). At the very summit of the building is a metal ornament consisting of the magic screen, the orb of the sun, the crescent, a ball for the other stars, and a piece of wire,

pointing upward into the Great Void, the vanity of all being. Round the Stupa runs a path of prayer lined with 108 small shrines.

Conflicting theories are still being put forward about the meaning and purpose of this edifice; and whether the shrine does in fact represent a human body is still hotly disputed. Because it consists of five components, it is held by some to represent the five elements: the base represents earth, the steps water, the dome fire, the cylinder the sky, and the ornament clear air. What is undisputed is that in the upper part of a Stupa something is immured, often the ashes or corpse of a Lama.

Leh obviously believes in religious toleration. It has a mosque with a minaret from which a muezzin calls the faithful to prayer, while behind the palace, just by the police-station, is a small church for the 200 or so Christians living in Ladakh.

The most prominent building in Leh is the 400 year-old royal palace, with its innumerable rooms, some of which are in an advanced stage of dilapidation; its faded and crumbling frescoes; and its wood-carvings, many of which have been purloined and used for fuel, and not only by invaders from Srinagar. Today this great palace is too dilapidated to be open to the public, but it still belongs to the royal family. Even during the lifetime of the last King, Rajah Kungsang Namgyal, who died as recently as 1974, the royal family resided in the palace only in March. When Ladakh was conquered and annexed by Kashmir in 1839, the Mahararah of Srinagar banished to Stok the heir to a dynasty that had lasted without interruption for close on a thousand years.

The 80-room palace in the small settlement about 8 kilometres from Leh on the other side of the river Indus is the residence of the late king's widow, Rani Parvati Devi Deskit Wangmo, but she uses a mere 12 rooms and

---

Pages 106/107   →
Leh today, a town set amid snow-covered mountains, with a place like the Potala in Lhasa. Leh has not changed very much in the last hundred years.

105

only in the summer, as there is no way of heating the building.

The Kings in Leh were mighty potentates and their independence was unchallenged. At one time or another their dominions stretched from Tibet to Kashmir and included such remote territories as Gilgit, Baltistan and Skardu. In battle they stood up to Mongols and Moguls and did not hesitate to change their religion if there was no other way of preserving their domains intact. So some of the Kings of Leh were Moslems: by no means all of them were Buddhists. But it was a King of Ladakh who finally proclaimed Buddhism the country's official religion.

The first King, Ske-id Ide Neiima Gon, from whom the present royal family are descended, was also a usurper. Before the start of the present dynasty's thousand years, power was in the hands of a different family. At the dawn of recorded history, for instance, there was one rejoicing in the name of Khri dPon bHag rDar Skei-abs. It was under one of his descendants, Singe Nomygal, that Ladakh attained its maximum expansion, and it was he who built the huge palace of Leh early in the 17th century. At the time when A. Reeve Heber and his wife Kathleen were exploring Ladakh there was still a king, but the British as well as the Maharajah of Kashmir had appointed a Governor or some other high-ranking official. On State occasions the standards of the King of Ladakh and the Maharajah of Kashmir fluttered side by side with the Union Jack. Heber describes a courtesy visit to the palace of Leh as follows: "Whenever the royal family moved to Leh in winter to attend the New Year festival, we politely enquired whether we could be received, and if so, what hour would be most convenient for their Majesties. Our application was usually accompanied by a gift of some kind, cabbages, turnips or potatoes, which are extremely expensive in this part of the world. Furthermore, the only places where they grew were our garden or on a patch behind the British Resident's house. A date and time for our audience having been agreed, we were conducted to the Queen's apartments and sat ourselves down quite close to her on a cushioned carpet . . . . . Butter tea was served, as well as cakes made in the royal kitchen. When the Queen heard that we were travelling she sent us some of these cakes wrapped in Indian newspaper as "something for the road", as she put it. The royal family are not very well off as they are only allowed to levy taxes in their place of exile, Stok. Their annual income must be about 4,000 rupees (about £ 300). Then the King came in, shook us by the hand and invited us to sit by him. Conversation flowed easily, as he had many questions to ask us and ready answers to our questions. The Queen joined in the conversation and complained that the King had no head for figures; she had to do all the accounts herself. The conversation kept turning to the circumstance that the King of Ladakh, who was now only allowed to call himself the Rajah of Stok, was by no means the only monarch hereabouts; in name at any rate there was still a King of Sangskar and a King of Marshro". In another passage Heber gives an account of his ride to Padum, the capital of Sangskar, where he encountered an old man who wanted to tell him something. The shabby-looking old man came to Heber's tent that evening with gifts of dried apricots and a handful of sugar. He turned out to be the last of a long line of Sangskar Kings and had lost his throne when resisting the Indian Moguls. The old man was now in difficulties: still regarding himself as his country's religious leader, he was anxious to rebuild the ruined monastery behind his house, but the Maharajah of Srinagar refused to believe him, fearing that the ex-King might fortify it and liberate his land from Kashmir occupation.

I too rode to Sangskar and met Nurbu, the heir to the throne, who in seven months had made pilgrimages with his father to Benares and Dharamsala, where the Dalai Lama is at present living. Even before reaching the village father and son were greeted by their "subjects": chang was served, and incense burning on small dishes gave off an appropriate aroma. To an accompaniment of oboes and beating drums the King seated himself on a carpet in the open air. It was touching to see how his dogs welcomed their master by jumping up at him, rolling over and over and barking ecstatically. More and more beer was served and the crowd became more and more animated, especially when three men executed a ceremonial dance with waving scarves. The whole thing was like a theatrical performance, with shining brown faces crowding round to catch a glimpse of their King and his son.

Later, I was invited to the King's house at Sangla. It is just like any other house there, only bigger. The entrance was so low that one had to bend almost double to pass through it: from there a dark passage of hard earth and uneven cobbles led up to a dirty curtain and the living-room. Here we sat down cross-legged and were served chang, followed by unsweetened tea. It was a room in which time seemed to have stood still. Schlagintweit and the Hebers must have sat where we were sitting, perhaps on the very same carpet; must have admired the same Thangkas on the walls. Only the old tea-service was no longer in evidence; the cups we drank from were "made in the People's Republic of China".

The Kings of Ladakh were the chief temporal authorities in the country, and since they too were re-incarnations they were also invested with a religious aura, as revealed in the person of the last survivor of the old dynasty, Tinlem Namgyal, the brother of the late King who died in 1974. Tinlem is now the administrator of Hemis monastery. His sister-in-law, the late King's widow, is still treated by the people as a sovereign queen. She is a re-incarnation of the goddess "White Drölma".

But to return to Leh: the houses cluster round an F-shaped thoroughfare, the "High Street" in which are situated the Post Office, a number at shops, the mosque, a bus-stop, two banks, a taxi-rank, and some small hotels. On either side of the street are ditches for irrigation purposes. Pedestrians either jump over them or use stepping-stones, of which there are far too few. The front-doors are never at street level but up one or two steps. This leaves room for the traders, beggars and visitors who congregate in the spaces between the steps and display their wares, cook their meals, and beg. The front-doors are made of thin wood and are left ajar so that women can quickly hide behind them if they see a stranger coming towards them with a camera. The side-streets are so narrow that there is barely room for two people to pass each other. Pedestrians frequently have to flatten themselves against a wall when a religious fanatic, absorbed in his devotions, comes wandering down the middle of the street swinging his prayer-wheel.

It is an animated street-scene: sturdy little horses loaded with dried yak-dung; women staggering breathlessly under bundles of wood which they hope to sell; shepherds with herds of sheep shouting their way through milling crowds; Ladakhis homeward bound in the evening with large bottles of chang; women wearing wide "peraks" (hats studded with precious stones) and enjoying a chat well away from each other because their lamb-skin ear-flaps are too bulky to permit a conversation at close quarters; and a wayside smith going about his fiery, noisy business. The bus for Srinagar stops at a corner and a customer wants to take his sheep with him, so the driver finds room for them on the roof with their legs tied together. So it would be a gross exaggeration to say that time has stood still in Ladakh: it is just that the clock is a little behind the times at latitude 34°10′N and longitude 77°40′E, 3,440 metres above sea-level and five kilometres north of the right bank of the Indus.

Finally, there is one European figure in stone who has been part of the Leh scene for over 100 years. An Austrian palaeontologist from Moravia named Ferdinand Stoliczka functioned from 1868 as Secretary of the Asiatic Society of Bengal and while exploring Ladakh arrived in Leh on 18 June 1874. After his death a statue was erected in his honour – the only statue in Leh.

*Leh seen from the
palace, looking down
on the Indus Valley
a small town, a strip
of green, and then
the vast expanse of
mountains.*

Stones
and Colours

The Lamas", wrote Alexander Cunningham in his book "Ladak", "arc unsurpassed, at least among Orientals, in the art of fashioning clay and metal". To these attributes should in my opinion be added a third, the art of blending the works of man with the works of Nature.

Covering the 16 kilometres from She monastery to Leh on foot, before coming in sight of the capital's outlying houses one passes a rock just taller than a man, and on it is inscribed in seven large red letters the prayer "Om mani padme hum". Graffiti in Tibet: some pilgrim or other felt the urge to harness Nature to his devotions and created a work of art out of an ordinary rockface (pages 118 and 119).

This is typical of Ladakh. Looking back, could Lamayuru monastery have been built anywhere but in the natural bowl in which it stands (page 30)? Could any military fastness be more discreetly half-hidden by its surroundings than Alchi monastery (pages 32 and 33)? Is not the great rock 1 kilometre beyond Mulbe the perfect setting for such a colossal statue (page 123), an 8 metres high likeness of Jampa, the god of grace? It is said to date from about the same time as the birth of Christ. In former times it was obviously possible to climb up to its head, as can be deduced from rectangular holes for hooks or rungs, but today a house built in 1975 obstructs access and blocks the view.

Even more striking examples of respect for the surrounding landscape are the "Mani", prayer-walls often many kilometres long. Not even in Tibet have I seen such long ones, and in Leh there are traces of complexes of walls laid out like city streets: their ritual negotiation must have taken hours.

"Mani" are the result of passing pilgrims piling up stones year after year until they attained the proportions of a waist or shoulder-high wall. Cunningham measured a "Mani" at Basgo 1.5 metres high, 3.6 metres thick, and 800 metres long, while the British traveller W. Moorcroft noted one almost a kilometre long in Leh, and dilapidated remains of it can still be seen today.

These prayer-walls are really altars on which the faithful have piled stones with prayers painted or scratched on them, usually the "Om mani padme hum". Most of these "prayers in stone" are requests for support in some undertaking or other and possess genuine artistic merit (page 127, above). Even an uninvolved stranger can activate them simply by passing along them without actually contributing to them. The great wall at Leh numbers many hundreds of thousand prayers, and merely walking along it greatly enhances the suppliant's prospects of a higher re-incarnation.

Sometimes a "Mani" is right in the middle of the road, a particularly good example being the one on the road to Alchi. This arrangement represents a very sensible compromise: it means that pilgrims going in either direction can walk along their own side of the Mani: red-caps on the right, yellow-caps on the left. Most of the stones are round at the sides and flat on top, and among them are some very valuable fossils, valuable because the faithful believe they fell from Heaven. There are also occasional stones with inscriptions not in Tibetan but in Sanskrit.

The prayers cover all kinds of different requests. A father yearns for a son, an itinerant trader hopes to return home safe and sound, a shepherd prays that his flocks will come to no harm during the icy winter. Moreover a Mani makes life easier for the suppliant by relieving him of all responsibility. Once he has deposited his stone on the wall he can turn his attention to other matters. As Cunningham puts it: "He returns home in the firm conviction that his prayer will be heard."

Some suppliants inscribe their own prayers, others have them inscribed at a monastery. Consequently there are professional Mani scribes just as there are professional Thangka painters, many of whom live at Palam, on the left bank of the Indus opposite the Tibetan refugee camp.

Art-historians have recently discovered that "Manis" were not started at random, just anywhere, but had a practical as well as a spiritual function, such as consolidating terraces or preventing landslides.

I myself came upon a strange group of pillars (page 127, bottom right) near the village of Dras, three rather angular obelisks of unequal height made of a sort of mica-shist like granite (the villagers call them "Chomo", goddesses). They have nothing whatever to do with Tibetan Buddhist art, and the inscriptions are in Kashmir Takri. Their height varies from 50 centimetres to 2 metres. On two of them are female figures with four arms, and on the smallest is a horseman with an inscription of 8 verses. These pillars are religious anachronisms in a neighbourhood that is governed by Islam. They are Buddhist sculptures (page 127, bottom right) and that they are nevertheless well cared for and looked after is another indication of Ladakhi tolerance.

But even Ladakhi tolerance does not go so far as to permit adherents of alien religions to erect or consecrate new images of Buddha, an undertaking which in its final stages involves some curious manoeuvres. No artist dares to look straight into Buddha's eyes, so how can he paint them? The solution is an ingenious one: the artist works with his back to the image and paints "blind" over his left shoulder.

Just as the "Manis" are still active on the suppliant's behalf long after he has safely settled down by his yak-dung fire, so too the elements play their part. The wind flutters the prayer-banners (page 136, top left), and streams rotate the prayer-wheels. The one illustrated on page 129, bottom left, is in a tiny little house near Karcha monastery in Sangskar. Water is a sort of perpetuum mobile: as well as being drunk by the monks and used for cooking, it drives prayer-wheels, thus dispatching prayers non-stop to the gods.

The wind is equally helpful, fluttering the prayer-banners on mountain-passes (page 58, top left); on roofs, rocks, and Stupas; above courtyards; or strung out on lines in the countryside (page 136, top left). These banners display rough drawings of symbolic animals: horses, tigers, lions and dragons, as well as inscriptions such as "May the teaching of Buddha prosper". The only colours permitted are blue, white, red, green and yellow, and the order in which they are arranged is strictly prescribed: blue, representing the sky; red, representing fire; white, representing water; green, representing fields and meadows; and yellow, representing earth.

Whereas prayer-banners are fairly plain and simple, "Thangkas" are extremely colourful and valuable. "Thangkas" can best be described as portable altar-paintings that can be rolled up, the outer surface being protected from damage by a curtain of silk. They are made of particularly precious material on which is painted in natural colours a representation of some element of Buddhist mythology. They are trimmed with brocade so that as well as allegorical paintings they can also illustrate cosmic components, – earth, air and sky.

In the lower half of a thangka is a rectangular piece of material of a different colour symbolising the pure water which is the origin of all things, as well as constituting a meditative "approach" to the painting.

"Thangkas" can be of enormous dimensions. In Hemis monastery there is one several metres long which in view of its size and value is only exhibited at a festival held every eleven years. The last time it was displayed on the facade of the main building was in 1969, so it is due to re-appear in 1980. Even the one which is exhibited at the annual mystery play at Hemis (page 163) is 6 x 10 metres, and it takes at least 4 monks to unroll it. Smaller ones owned by the monks are usually about 65 x 30 centimetres. The Swiss explorer Pierre Vittoz made a detailed study of Ladakhi painting, and the following are extracts from the conclusions he formed.

"The choice of material, the best time to start on a painting, the style and proportions of the individual components – all these details are laid down in the holy scriptures and traditional precepts to which the artist must rigidly adhere. The religious importance of paintings lies in the fact that nearly all of them are ritually consecrated and classified as sacred. The most famous of them are popularly believed to be of supernatural origin; either they just came into being or they fell from Heaven".

Although most compositions have a certain similarity about them, several of them can claim distinct artistic merit due to the firmness of the ductus and the harmony of their colours. To understand them, one needs to know a good deal about Hindu as well as Buddhist theology and ritual.

A feature of Leh is a penthouse perched above the main street. The covered structure in the bottom right-hand corner was intended (but never used) for policemen on point-duty: today it is just somewhere where pedestrians can sit down for a moment or two.

Page 115
What looks so enormous from close to looks minute from a distance: Tiktse Monastery.

Vittoz continues: "Some techniques have even found their way over the Himalayas. A dreamy-looking eye, for instance, is portrayed exactly as in Indian art, shaped like a delightfully curved lip".

Paintings are usually done on cotton, linen or silk. The painter mounts his "canvas" in a wooden frame and applies a thin coating of starch which is then smoothed with a small piece of wood or a flat stone. The essential guide-lines are drawn by a bamboo stick dipped in charcoal. The result is like a geometrical pattern which can still be traced in the completed painting, with axes, circles, triangles and parallels. Outlines are usually applied by a stencil studded with holes. The colours used to be extracted from plants and minerals, but for some time now they have been imported in powder form from India and are mixed with glue.

"Long firm lines" writes Vittoz, "accentuate the contours. The figures and the folds in their robes are reproduced by soft, continuous lines which underline their expansive gestures. An urgent, imperious movement is depicted by rounded hips and arms and streaming hair." There is little other content to distract the eye from the central figure. "The artist forgoes elaboration" says the Indian Madanjid Singh in his book "Himalayan art", but prefers to allow his figures to make their effect in a barren environment. As a spiritual and material counterbalance to a raging monster, for instance, there is a plain block of granite, symbolising indestructible wisdom and capable of outliving demons as well as human beings. As Vittoz puts it: "The colours are vivid and highly contrasted, yet so skilfully juxtaposed that they never clash. This interplay of bright, warm shades of red, gold, green and violet, delineated more by dividing lines than by varying depths of shadows, has something about it that is so decisive, radiant and at the same time simple, that it bears a curious resemblance to the technique and impact of our best glass-painting".

One of the painter's most important duties is the depiction of the "wheel of life", which is intended to illustrate the hardships and misery of earthly life and the sufferings of those who cling to it, as opposed to the bliss of Nirvana. The wheel is held fast in the teeth and claws of the beast "worldly joys", and its hub is decorated with animals symbolising lust, envy, hate and stupidity, namely the cock, the serpent and the pig. It is these vices that keep the wheel revolving. It has 6 sectors, representing mortal life. It also illustrates the world-weariness of the gods, who as prisoners of the wheel are not immortal; the anger of the demi-gods who hope to make their way to Paradise; human diseases and old age; the torture of animals; the sufferings of (apparently) Tantalus, who is being strangled; and the terrors of the 16 hells.

Nearby is a seated figure of Buddha, safe and aloof from the torments depicted in the wheel, laughing and pointing to the road to eternal bliss.

"The Buddhas", writes Pierre Vittoz, "float in glorioles, and in the simplicity of their features there is something mysterious and illuminating. There could be no greater contrast than that between the Buddhas and the angry gods with their podgy bodies, distorted, plump arms, oversized, flat-nosed faces, saucer-eyes, and leering mouths with long, crooked fangs. Several of them have serpents writhing in their hair and necklaces of human bones, besides being armed with a sword and trident. The predominent colours are red, bluish-green, and indigo. Paintings of this kind may seem to us grotesque, but the vitality of the depiction is eloquent testimony to the skill of those who painted them and to the vividness of their apocalyptic visions. These artists succeed in reproducing a veritable witches' sabbath of unrestrained brutality, not to mention details such as being roasted alive or disembowelled, and positively sadistic portrayals of frostbite and frozen feet".

Symbolism looms large, one essential feature being the lotus. Immensely enlarged, they serve the gods as thrones; immensely reduced, as jewels on their fingers. Other highly symbolic features are lightnings, magic daggers, and glorioles. Among the physical abnormalities of the gods are eleven heads, four arms and a thousand hands, each of which has an eye as a symbol of omnipresence, watchfulness, power, and sympathy.

So much for "thangkas". In Ladakh, however, artists specialised in, and perfected, another form of painting, namely frescoes. Madanjid Singh devotes particular attention to Alchi monastery, which possesses frescoes dating from the 11th to the 17th centuries, which means that some of them are nearly a thousand years old (though the monastery itself is half as old again). These frescoes are still as vivid as if they had been painted yesterday (pages 131, left; and 133, below); they are often several metres wide and are strangely impressive. Only in such dry air could the brilliance of the colours survive, some of the rooms containing them being open on one side.

Alchi is a half-forgotten masterpiece consisting of a complex of all sorts of buildings, a labyrinth of Stupas, garden walls, temples, and dark rooms (usually closed) containing Buddhas that have their feet on the floor and their heads somewhere on the third floor, which is reached by "ladders" of notched beams. Nearly all Alchi's gables are decorated with wood-carvings painted red, some of which are in very bad condition (page 132). A snow-leopard is seated on a triangular gable in which the elephant-god Ganesh is enthroned on a lotus. Something I had never seen before were the "Tsatsas" on the wall of the temple at Alchi (page 126). "Tsatsas" are small clay statuettes of gods which always incorporate a grain of rice or barley, and occasionally some of the ashes of a Lama. There are thousands of Tsatsas in Stupas, tombs and memorial shrines. They can be compared perhaps with our votive offerings, and Alexander Cunningham, the most accurate historian of Ladakh, counted 30 cubic metres of Tsa-tsas in a precinct of the temple of Nako. Each piece was 3 centimetres high and inscribed on the reverse side with the word "Tsa" (medallion). On a wall of the temple at Alchi are about 200 of these miniature sculptures, and although they are guarded by a ferocious-looking demon, the abbot allowed me to choose two of them for myself. Today they still hang on a wall, albeit a few thousand kilometres from the original one, namely in my home.

Travelling up from Srinagar and turning south-east into the Indus valley at Khalatse,

before tackling the final 97 kilometres to Leh, one notices increasing numbers of what must be the world's most curious headgear in existence, the "Perak", (pages 134 and 135).

Its history might well begin with the words "Once upon a time". Once upon a time a King of Ladakh married the daughter of a prince who ruled a far-off country, and she brought to her new home a "Perak", which the women of Ladakh immediately took to copying. Since those days the headgear has been not only attractive but has become a "status symbol" of prosperity and social standing, and in present-day Leh a "Perak" could cost up to £ 500. A particularly good example of one is illustrated on page 57. A "Perak" consists of a long strip of leather running down the back of the neck and shoulders and coming to a pointed end just above the waist. The front end, just above the bridge of the nose, is also pointed, because tradition has it that the strip of leather is meant to represent a snake. The two lamb-skin ear-flaps enhance this impression: seen from the front the whole "Perak" really does look like an infuriated cobra about to strike. The leather is covered with red cloth on to which generations of women have sewn uncut turquoises ("Per" is the old Ladakhi word for turquoise). The front end of a "Perak" is usually ornamented with a particularly fine precious stone, often gold. Particularly costly ones have a cornelian on the crown of the head, and the "tail" hanging down the back is often sewn with silver and gold amulets. Originally there were no ear-flaps, but according to the legend they were added because one of the Queens of Ladakh used to get earache. Obviously the ladies of the court had to fall in with the new fashion and eventually it not only became firmly established but also introduced a new hair-style: the women made long plaits of each other's hair and then sewed them on to the ear-flaps.

On the left side of the "Perak", starting from just above the shoulder is a horizontal silver ornament from which hang several strings of red corals. On the right side, further silver ornaments of various shapes and sizes are fastened to the hair: some women sport them on both sides. In country districts only one or two strings of corals are worn (page 135, bottom

"Graffiti" by some devout pilgrim on the road from Leh to Tiktse: the words are those of the prayer "Om mani padme hum" ("O jewel in the lotus flower").

right), whereas in Leh some "Peraks" are so heavy that the ornaments are attached to a wide black band under the shoulders. The widow of the last King possesses a superb one nearly half a metre wide with 450 turquoises. Most women take off the middle part of a "Perak" before going to bed, but the ear-flaps are retained because they are sewn on to the hair: they are only removed when the women wash their hair. In former times girls started collecting turquoises at the age of five or six and supplemented them with cowry shells, which married women were not allowed to wear. A "Perak" was deemed to be part of a girl's trousseau: savings were invested in one, and a widow could eke out a living by selling off the stones. Most of the "Peraks" one sees in Leh today are heirlooms. The mother has to hand over her "Perak" to her eldest daughter as a wedding-present and make do with a more modest one for her own use. For political as well as financial reasons the custom of using sable for the ear-flaps instead of lambskin is no longer observed, because the sable used to be imported from Jarkand, which is now part of Chinese East Turkestan. The only person who still wears an inherited sable "Perak" is the Queen.

Considering what a poor country Ladakh is, the wealth of jewellery worn by the women is astonishing. Apart from the adornments already described, they deck themselves out with heavy gold or silver necklaces (page 134, bottom centre) and all kinds of rings and amulets (page 134, top left), not to mention leather-belts hung with cowry shells from some sea-coast thousands of kilometres away. On their ears are wire loops set with tiny pearls, and round their wrists are bracelets of shells which are jangled as a form of greeting. Perhaps the most curious adornments are silver necklaces of tiny little brushes, bodkins, tweezers for removing unsightly hairs, and minute scoops for extracting wax from the ears. To a more modest extent jewellery is worn by men too, but decently concealed under thick coats: amber, turquoise and coral necklaces, and open-ended brass bangles with snakes' heads at each end. Both men and women favour the same headgear, a sort of top-hat with

vertical seams and woven patterns, the brim folded slightly back on either side of the forehead (page 135, middle: pages 50, 51 and 54, bottom left). In 1977 a hat of this kind could be bought in Leh for the equivalent of about £ 5, which is one reason why it is gradually ousting the far more beautiful but much too elaborate "Perak".

Apart from coral and cowry shells, which had to be imported, all these precious stones and metals are indigenous to Ladakh, so these elaborate hats are not so surprising as they might at first seem. Silver and copper are mined in the mountains, and there is gold in the River Indus. And in the words of the British missionary Heber "turquoise is often found hereabouts".

Other adornments which are almost as elaborate as the "Perak" and are worn only by the "black hat" dancers who perform at monastery festivals and mystery plays are wraps made of human bones. It often takes a craftsman a whole lifetime to carve all the thunderbolts, likenesses of gods, bells and "good-luck" symbols out of material that gets darker and darker all the time (page 131, detail). These wraps cover the whole body and are so richly elaborated with ornaments for the forehead, arms and feet that they can weigh several kilograms. They are very jealously guarded by the monasteries, and I have never succeeded in getting my hands on more than a fragment or two for my collection of "Tibetiana".

Several monasteries attach the utmost importance to valuable books and manuscripts and there are some wonderful libraries in Ladakh, notably at Lamayuru and Tiktse monasteries. Many of the books are hand-written and illustrated. The library at Lamayuru is next to the refectory, and the abbot took great pride in showing me the complete "Kanjur", the Sacred Books, and the "Tanjur", the commentary thereon. These are the fundamental tenets of Tibetan Buddhism, a total of 360 volumes incorporating over 1,000 works. Several books are a thousand pages long and weigh from five to ten kilograms without their elaborate wooden covers, which is why it takes twenty yaks to transport the Sacred Books of Tibet. In former times these books were written by hand: now they are printed, only the blocks of each individual page must be carved out of birch-wood, each letter being set as if reflected in a mirror. The blocks are then coloured, and the pages (which are of paper made from daphne laureola) are spread over them and pressed down with the ball of the thumb. As the books consist entirely of religious matter and pictures of saints, the process is illuminated by butter-lamps. The books are stored in a complex of square pigeon-holes, the pages are attached to wooden covers by strips of cloth and wrapped in silk. The pigeon-holes of the magnificent old library at Tiktse monastery are lined with gold.

Travellers in Ladakh have always been amazed by the curious garments hanging out to dry on clothes-lines, etc. Some of the trousers exposed to view must belong to a race of giants, with legs two metres long. It is even more astonishing to find that these garments belong to females. It is the same with men's shirts, which have sleeves 1½ to 2 metres long. Yet the Ladakhis one sees in public never seem to be wearing outsize trousers or shirts. The explanation is simple: they wear these immense garments like concertinas: the surplus length is folded into overlaps, and the resulting void between skin and air acts as a sort of insulation against extreme cold in winter and extreme heat in summer. Moreover, long sleeves are an indication that the owner of the garment in question is not obliged to work with his hands. Cosmetics are traditionally unknown, apart from the practice of painting the body against evil spirits, the sun, and disease. The few examples of make-up that I encountered were primarily cures for head-aches, darkening of the skin and "stirrings of the humours of the body": the women had painted tiny yellow and black spots on the upper half of their faces with herbal extracts or tar-ointment.

More attention is paid to the long hair worn by both sexes, yet even long hair is gradually giving way to the more practical short hair enjoined by the army. In the villages one still sometimes sees men laying their heads on wooden blocks for the women to wash their menfolk's hair (once a month) in soda (which is readily available everywhere in the form of borax) and warm water. The men's hair is then smeared with apricot or mustard oil and plaited with wool into a pigtail that leaves unsightly marks on the wearer's coat of green or red wool. These voluminous overcoats accommodate not only human beings: men in particular have converted them into mobile wardrobes into which they cram anything that could come in handy during the day. With his capacious overcoat and its assorted contents a Ladakhi male is self-sufficient: he can survive accidents and long treks across the high mountains, and has nothing to fear from the desert. He also equips himself with a small leather bag edged with metal and containing flint and tinder. Of course he could perfectly well buy matches in Leh, but matches go out, whereas the traditional way of producing fire is less fallible. All he has to do is hold the flint in one hand and with the other strike the tinder with the metal edge of his leather bag, and, lo and behold, he has fire!

Another highly important accessory stored in overcoats is a knife, even if it is only a cheap mass-produced one, though not infrequently it is a home-made tool with a heavy wooden handle. The sheath is often inlaid with coral and turquoise, though nowadays cheap beads are more common.

Two other indispensable items of a Ladakhi's equipment are a long spoon and a sewing-kit. From a distance, the latter looks like a round or square piece of leather, just thick enough to fit conveniently into the palm of one's hand. From each side protrudes a piece of string. The outer surface is often elaborately ornamented with small stones or coloured thread. A pull on the shorter end of the string discloses the contents of the bag carefully arranged in a sort of drawer: a needle, thread, and a small bodkin which is often made of a musk-deer's horn. I remember once in a side-street in Leh meeting a caravan-leader wearing a vast woollen coat fastened round his middle with a belt. Hidden under the top half of the coat was a weird medley of belongings, and the purpose of the belt was to prevent them falling about his feet. Among them was a 40 centimetre long flute which he had made himself and enjoyed playing during his lonely journeys. The flute in

Page 122
This golden statue of Buddha adorns a darkened hall in one of Ladakh's monasteries. The body is draped with brocade and the crown is studded with large precious stones.

This statue of the god Jampa hewn out of the rock-face about 1 kilometre from Mulbe is over eight metres high. The prayer-banners on top of the rock were placed there by pilgrims.

no way restricted his movements, nor had I even spotted a bulge under his coat. In fact there seems to be no way of detecting how much a Ladakhi has concealed about his person. One often sees people rummaging in their coats up to the elbows, and all that emerges is a plug of tobacco, or tweezers for tweaking hairs out of their noses. On the other hand I have seen a man extricate a howling baby from his coat and hand it over to its mother.

Nowadays more and more of the good old unpractical utensils are being replaced by thoroughly practical, thoroughly up-to-date and thoroughly ugly products. Up to a few years ago every Ladakhi carried a home-made wooden cup in his coat. Today, these cups have given way to plastic mugs and enamel saucers. The lovely old mirrors of polished brass are today found only in museums and antique shops, and the womenfolk use fragments of glass broken off from an ordinary wall-mirror.

Alchi Monastery: the faithful are allowed to take down these clay statues of gods and hand-painted votive offerings from the walls, but a demon ensures that no unauthorised person is allowed access.

Above: a "Mani" wall. In Ladakh some of these extraordinary walls are many kilometres long. They consist of an accumulation of stones, painted or inscribed with religious texts, and deposited by passing pilgrims.

Below left – These spears and lances on the roof of Tiktse Monastery are supposed to ward off evil spirits and protect the monks from all harm.

Below right – These Buddhist obelisks near the village of Dras are nevertheless respected as symbols of an alien religion.

Spirits and Demons

Ladakh has been called the "Land of Smiles". It could also be called the land of spirits and demons, of magic rituals to ward them off, and of witchcraft. The conflict between good and evil is unceasing. A man must be on his guard against the powers of evil twenty-four hours a day, and at almost every step a traveller in Ladakh will come across mystic signs on walls and roofs, and even inside houses, designed to protect the inmates against evil spirits. People actually take steps to protect spirits against demons. In Sangskar I came upon a sheep's head impaled upon a pole and mummified by the dry air, that was supposed to watch over a small room haunted by a spirit (page 147, bottom left). The head was wrapped in prayer-banners, and pieces of coloured cloth round the pole were also meant to ward off evil demons. There is a similar but even larger head in a narrow street near the royal palace in Leh, that of an Ovis Ammon (a Tibetan wild sheep) with branching horns, mounted above the front-door architrave and painted in lurid colours. Nothing would induce the owners of the house to sell it; it was a protection, they insisted, against illness as well as evil spirits. Ladakhis feel they are constantly at the mercy of supernatural powers whose existence is not doubted for a moment. Nor will they embark upon the slightest project without first consulting the gods. Journeys are postponed, family feasts are cancelled, and even important administrative measures are held up pending the approval of "oracles". In Sangskar I was once able to observe what happens when a family calls in one of these "oracles" (pages 138/139 and 142/143). He was an elderly man who "practised" at Sangla and promised the villagers he could at least diagnose diseases if not actually cure them. In no time at all ten women turned up with their children for "consultations", but the "oracle" was not quite ready. Seating himself on a carpet behind a painted table he started imbibing copious draughts of Tibetan beer, with a shawl round his shoulders and a sort of crown made of five different pieces of cloth on his head. He then knelt down in silence in front of the table, glanced from time to time at a box of amulets (page 138, bottom left), and prayed for about 15 minutes.

This man was just an ordinary practitioner, not one of the great "national" oracles or seers who are consulted on matters affecting whole countries and populations, and who are subjected to immense mental and physical strains, which is why the majority of them do not live long. Another factor contributing to their early decease may well be the strong drugs they use to induce a speedier and deeper state of trance. This oracle at Sangla contented himself with drinking a lot of beer and uttering short, declamatory prayers. The beer was handed to him at regular intervals by a young assistant while the crowd of patients and onlookers waited for the oracle to be possessed by a spirit. As a guest, I had to be careful to be as tactful and unobtrusive as possible. I was anxious to take some photographs of his "treatment" and had to be careful not to give the impression that I regarded the whole procedure as a fraud, particularly as the Ladakhis were profoundly moved and waited devoutly for the oracle to go into a trance.

All at once the oracle began to tremble all over. His hands and legs twitched convulsively, the "crown" fell off his head, the upper part of his body stiffened, and he clutched his head in both hands. With a loud groan he half rose to his feet, stamped his feet, and suddenly fell to the ground. The spirit he had conjured up had taken possession of him. Now at last he made a sign that he was ready to deal with his patients. "Oracle" is perhaps not the right word for these healers. They can be miracle-workers, wizards, shamans, or just charlatans. In certain circumstances they are also able to answer questions relating to the future. While in trance they can interpret omens and foretell what the next two or three days will bring. At any rate they make pretensions to be able to do so, and what is more important, the Ladakhis believe them. Curiously enough the patients were all women (page 138, page 139 bottom left, pages 142 and 143), among them the Queen of Sangskar. I noticed a flat silver pan containing some water, and as the "treatment" proceeded I could see what it was for. Patients have to sit down on a carpet in front of the healer and describe their

Ladakh boasts an astonishing wealth of treasures – and considerable ingenuity in exploiting them, as is illustrated by this prayer-wheel in Karcha Monastry: it is rotated by water-power and was once used for storing motor-oil.
Right: the White Lion of Tibet serving as a chapiter in Alchi Monastery.

On a wooden plaque in Hemis Monastery is inscribed a letter from Lhasa enjoining visitors to behave with due respect in this sacred edifice.

A beautiful old Thangka in Gö-Tsang, a retreat high above Hemis Monastery, portraying the life of Buddha.

Left – There are an almost infinite variety of frescoes in Ladakh. These two on the left come from Hemis and Thiktse Monasteries.

Right – Detail of an apron made of human bones: it is worn by performers in mystery plays

131

Three Stupas below
Karcha Monastery.
The spikes are used
for flying
prayer-banners.
Below, left: Likeness
of Buddhist gods
carved on a cleft
rock near She.
Below, right: A
woodcut of the
Tibetan lion in Alchi
Monastery.

The Tibetan lion
again: above, on the
main Stupa in Leh;
and below, in a
fresco in Alchi
Monastery.

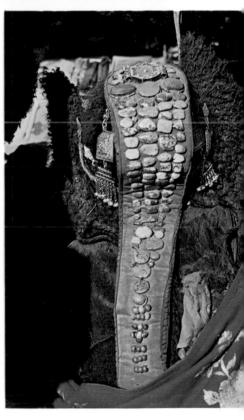

Rings, hats, necklaces, costly materials: the women of Ladakh, like women the world over, love finery. And jewellery is also a good investment. The coral and turquoise ornaments on their peculiar headgear are heirlooms that have been handed down for generations and indicate the social status of the wearer. The gold comes from the country's rivers, and the silver from its mines; whereas the coral has been imported from Italy for centuries.

Most of Ladakh's works of art are made of gold, silver, wood, silk, brocade and linen. For this large statue of Buddha at She, where the size of the figure is beyond the resources of the monastery or village concerned, copper is also used. As for the numerous prayer-banners, the favourite colour is blue, followed by white, red, green and yellow. Below right: the pioneer of Ladakh's suspension bridges.

symptoms, explaining where the evil had entered their bodies and established itself inside. Several women indicated their breasts or knees and exposed them. The ensuing "treatment" provoked a wide variety of reactions among the women. Some went into a sort of ecstasy, with distorted grimaces, mouths wide open (ready to scream) and eyes tightly closed (page 143). Others appeared to be in pain, groaning and clenching their teeth. A few stayed quite still and assumed an air of devout expectation as if concentrating on deriving the maximum benefit from the "treatment", i. e. the expulsion of an infectious evil by the oracle possessed by a spirit.

As soon as the patients had indicated where the infection was, the oracle bent down and began to suck the skin with such vehemence that (as I could see with my own eyes) arteries sometimes burst with a great rush of blood. No wonder some of the patients' faces were contorted with pain. Nevertheless the oracle kept feeling the affected part with his finger-tips, just like a doctor, and resumed the suction, at the same time emitting a loud hissing noise, obviously to impress the bystanders. But every time he paused for breath I could see that he was not nearly in such a deep trance as he pretended to be. He knew perfectly well that I was photographing him as I had previously asked his permission and placed a couple of rupee notes on his little table. Presently he stole a quick glance in my direction to see if I was still there with my camera. Eventually I climbed over him to take a close-up of his head and the contorted features of his victim (page 143). Whatever it was that the healer claimed to have sucked out of his patient, he first retained it in his mouth, then turned and spat it out into the silver pan (page 139, bottom right). If the patient was still not satisfied that she was cured, the treatment was resumed all over again until at last the healer diagnosed the patient's condition from the spittle in the pan and prescribed what she had to do to cure herself.

The oracle refused to let me go without foretelling me the future of my expedition. There could be one or two difficulties, he opined, but everything would be all right in the end, and in fact this was exactly what happened.

After dealing with his patients (and me) the healer was completely exhausted, falling forward on to his carpet as if he had been struck dead, and while he was being attended to by his assistants the assembled patients observed complete silence.

There are any number of oracles in Ladakh, some amateur, some professional. Most of them live in villages and are prepared to show what they can do whenever called upon, but a small minority travel from village to village like itinerant medicine-men. At She there is an oracle who from time to time mounts his horse and offers prophecies in the neighbouring villages. Before starting, he gives himself over to at least 48 hours of prayer. He is venerated as a god and is firmly believed to be endowed with supernatural powers, whereas other people claiming to be able to foretell the future are looked down upon, notably at Tiktse and Stok, for instance, where oracles do not enjoy high social standing, though they are feared because of their accomplishments. The two oracles at Stok differ from others in that they only appear in public on certain appointed dates: whether they like it or not, they are bound to offer their services on the 9th and 10th days of the third month. In Malho there lives an oracle who has no hesitation in displaying his powers to all and sundry. He is a priest, lives in the monastery, and on his appointed days wanders around in the mountains blindfolded and carrying on his chest and back two paintings through which he "sees". Eventually he seats himself by a spring at the foot of the hill on which the monastery is built and is at his "customers'" disposal. But Ladakh's leading oracle is an old man in Tiktse who "speaks" through others. He is said to have effected miraculous cures on animals as well as human beings, but instead of sucking out the infection with his mouth, like the healer at Sangskar, he uses a tube. And of course he too can foretell the future. Rolf Schettler, the writer of the best guide to Ladakh, reports that in 1975 the old man initiated a new oracle, a young woman from Leh married to a joiner: even in her teens she was famous for her reliability as a medium.

The Ladakhis resort to innumerable methods of protecting themselves against spirits and

Shaman healers claim to be able to effect miraculous cures. After drinking Tibetan beer they go into a trance until their bodies are racked and possessed by a healing spirit. After touching the affected part of the sufferer's body the shaman sucks the infection out and expectorates it into a silver bowl filled with water (page 139, bottom right). The sufferer (page 138 bottom right), in this case the Queen of Sangskar, becomes extremely agitated, whether from pain or ecstasy is a matter of opinion.
See also pages 142 and 143.

demons. By painting the corners of their houses red they ensure that their homes are inviolable; but if the presence of good spirits (which do exist) is desired, the walls must be daubed with white crescents.

In short, there is not a single element of Ladakhi life that cannot, or ought not, to be protected, and precautions are taken even before birth. Even an embryo in the womb is menaced by 100,000 demons with 24 perils that only a Lama can avert by declaiming passages from books of exorcism, performing magic gestures, swinging a thunderbolt and ringing the magic bell. As soon as the child is born its forehead is disfigured with soot because spirits are only attracted by pretty babies.

To avert the evil eye a piece of paper inscribed (if possible by a Lama) with magic formulas is sewn into a small woollen bag and attached to the headgear as an amulet. There is a different kind of protection for every kind of danger so that adolescents often have ten to twenty of these coloured bags attached to their clothing. For perfect protection the Ladakhis turn to the local smith, who after being given a good meal is asked to let the child sit on his lap, so that the child absorbs the smell of the smith, an odour which evil spirits are said to abominate. The German missionary S. H. Ribbach, who spent twenty years in Ladakh, described in his book "Drogpa Nangyal" what happens when a father asks a soothsayer to set up a horoscope for a new-born baby. After laboriously spending over twenty years (1892–1913) collecting details of this procedure Ribbach wrote: "In his cramped dark cell, black with smoke, that clings to the steep rockface like a swallow's nest, sits the astrologer and soothsayer Dordje Dudjoms. By fasting, meditation, magic formulas and gestures he has just brought under control and conjured up his tutelary demon, the terrible Tamdrin, so vividly that he is convinced he can see him standing before him in human guise. In his state of ecstasy he is subjected to the process of Yoga, the mystic union with his tutelary demon, who is now obedient to his orders and bereft of his magic powers. Next, the astrologer takes down from a shelf some ancient tables and spreads them out on the little table in front of him. Among the tables, filthy with the marks

of constant consultation, is the likeness of a tortoise, and on the shell covering his stomach is an astrological calendar giving the animal signs for each year of the twelve-year cycle, as well as other beasts, monsters, magic signs and figures, among them the "Sparka" sign, a pattern of continuous and broken lines, and the nine "Meva" signs, rectangles with figures and the names of each of the five "elements" (fire, water, earth, wood and iron) in their respective colours: red, blue, yellow, green and white. Next to the calendar is a large astrological table on linen divided like a chessboard into squares of different colours, each denoting one of the five "elements". The astrologer's eyes are fixed on his tables and his dirty fingers grope for a pile of discs rather like draughtsmen which he then arranges on the coloured squares and moves them from side to side, or up and down, in accordance with some magic ritual, until some of the squares are completely full. Next, he turns his attention to the calendar with the animal-signs and keeps up a sort of subdued murmur while his eyes and fingers range over the magic numbers. 'Fire is a child of wood, which sustains it: the connection is harmless. But see here: monkey and tiger! These are bitter enemies and this is an evil omen! The years in which mother and child were born do not accord with their animal-signs, and that means a visitation by evil spirits'. Now he extracts from a dirty old leather bag a number of black and white discs made of horn and arranges them in two separate piles. Suddenly his eyes flash: 'The earth-dagger that keeps spirits under control has been wrenched out of the ground! Woe unto you, son of . . .! The spirits of earth and water are at large and will torment you! And see here: the Meva signs bode ill, the elements are in conflict with each other, the demons and witches of the mountains are raving. Wait a moment, my son: I will write you a formula! So saying, he takes a long strip of paper, and still sitting on his little carpet, holds the paper in his left hand and writes down what the stars and his magic signs and figures, not to mention his fertile imagination, have revealed to him about his little son's prospects. 'This boy was born in a wood and tiger year, whereas his mother was born in a fire and monkey year. Fire and wood are compatible, but tiger and monkey are enemies. The powers of evil are stronger than the powers of good.' He then proceeds to draw on his paper little circles denoting good signs, and crosses denoting bad signs, corresponding to the black and white discs. From the Sparka row he withdraws the sign for earth. This makes things even worse. More rings and crosses are drawn, the latter at first predominating; but other secret signs are added, and the preponderance of crosses is diminished until by the end of the first procedure the good signs are in the ascendant – soon he is writing again: "The signs for the boy's physical future, and for his power and fortune, are good: those for his life and intelligence less good. The rope connecting earth and heaven is broken: the earth-dagger has been wrenched out of the ground. The powerful spirits of the earth and their queen, along with the mighty water-gods are unleashed and infuriated! They can only be appeased by building a number of small clay stupas, by baking a huge votive cake for the queen of the earth. For the water-gods that dwell in the streams and springs of the village, pellets of dough are to be strewn upon the waters as votive offerings. Beware of building a house or digging up the ground during the coming year! Neither grow nor eat turnips! After sunset do not walk over a freshly ploughed field! Do not walk in a south-westerly or north-easterly direction! The book of the Ten Thousand Water-Gods must be read in your house! Make cross-wires to close the portals of heaven and earth against demons and witches!' At this point the soothsayer drops some ink from his copper ink-well on to the balls of his thumbs and with this rough and ready "ink-pad" imprints his signet under what he has written, which he then wraps in a covering of silk. Now he has finished. With a smile of satisfaction he rolls up the future prospects of an unwitting child into a scroll ready to be handed over to the anxious father".

Of course there are other less complicated (and less expensive) methods of ascertaining the future and securing protection against evil spirits. One can learn what is in store for one from the shoulder-blade of a sheep, from dice,

and from consulting a "rosary". And demons can be appeased by a modest offering of beer and barley. In my book "Geister und Dämonen" I described various devices adopted by Ladakhis, Nepalese and Tibetans for their protection, devices which are also not uncommon in other parts of the world; for instance, the doll suspended from the eaves and wielding a bow and arrow (page 146), though in this particular case the protection has lost most of its effectiveness as the bow has slipped out of position. Even commoner devices are animals, in this illustration (page 147) an enormous mastiff and a sheep's head. The mastiff is stuffed with straw and hangs above the front-door. On the roof of Ridzong monastery is a trident impaled in a human skull (page 147). On the roof of Tiktse monastery is a bundle of spears and lances to ward off evil spirits (page 127, bottom left). The monks assured me that these were exactly the kind of spears the spirits used themselves, so they were being repaid in their own coin!

Goethe opined that superstition is the poetry of life. If he was right, then Ladakh must be one of the most poetic places on earth. There is a nice story of how a Yogi's prophecies were distorted by a goddess. It is an example of the belief that a human being is merely a plaything of supernatural powers, but that in the end his destiny lies in his own hands as long as he believes that he can control spirits and demons. "Rechung, a pupil of the celebrated sage and scribe Milarepa, was ordered by his master to fast for seven days, after which he would meet on the market-square a Yogi named Tipu. 'You will easily recognise him' said Milarepa 'because his face is blue and the whites of his eyes are red. He will be dressed in an antelope-skin and will be blowing a trumpet pointed heaven-wards'. Rechung duly found Tipu, who prophesied that Rechung would be dead in 14 days. When Rechung returned to Milarepa with this dreadful news, the latter confessed that he had known it all along, but added that there was one way of defeating the prohecy: Rechung must fast another 7 days and then make a

→

Page 142/143; see page 139

pilgrimage to the goddess 'Ma chig grube rgyalmo' who alone could prolong his life despite Tipu's prophecy. Rechung did as he was bid and was received by the goddess, who asked him how long he thought of living. Rechung replied 'Until I have no wish to go on living'. The goddess granted his request and confided to him the secret of eternal life, a secret which has been handed down by the initiated right up to the present day. Rechung lived to be 88, exactly the same age as his master Milarepa had been when he died."

The Festivities at Hemis

No account of Ladakh would be complete without a description of the annual festivities at the great monasteries. The most lavish and spectacular of them all is the Mystery Play at Hemis, famous for its grotesque and elaborate costumes. The Tibetans call it "Drugpa Tsechu", which means that it takes place on the tenth day of the sixth month of the Ladakh calendar, i. e. in June or July. It is held on the birthday of Padme Sambhava, the founder of the Tibetan form of Buddhism and head of the Red Cap sect. There are two versions of his origin: in Sikkim he is said to have been a redoubtable magician who came to Tibet during the 7th century and succeeded in convincing the Lamas that he was a reincarnation of Buddha. Other Buddhists however maintain that he was responsible for introducing the old "Bön" religion with its worship of the devil and sensual delights. He is said to have encouraged his followers to eat meat and drink wine as only after material appetites had been appeased could a state of absolute abstraction be achieved.

In the years when the Ladakhi lunar calendar means that the festivities take place in what we call June, few tourists can negotiate the snow still blocking the Sochi Pass. Starting from Leh however one follows the River Indus upstream, turning left after 30 kilometres and crossing a brigde into a lateral valley. The main road ends 20 minutes before Hemis, so we joined the pilgrims making their way to the monastery on foot from all parts of the country. The monastery is half-hidden by a huge projecting wall of rock, and the path up to it, lined with long stone walls and white stupas, winds past terraced fields seamed with long rows of poplars and willows. As we drew nearer to Hemis we were enchanted by the lovely pastel tints of the landscape – the mild greyish-brown of the rocks, the pale green of the early foliage, the dazzling white of the stupas, and the pink of their roofs. And then all of a sudden the monastery came into full view, a broad, lofty building flanked by the monks' quarters, small houses built into the rock-face. The air was heavy with the scent of wild-roses. The precincts of the monastery were a hive of activity accompanied by music, laughter and scraps of conversation. Beneath the welcome shade of spreading trees small tents had been erected and the smoke of numerous fires ascended vertically into an azure blue sky (as wood is very scarce in Ladakh, the pilgrims brought their own fuel with them). And as some 3,000 of them had made the long laborious pilgrimage to Hemis, to say that the precincts were overcrowded would be a considerable understatement.

The occasion is not purely a religious one, it is also a sort of fair, with booths and stands offering food, tea, jewellery and wood. One of the most densely crowded was the stall dispensing beer, and one or two smart opportunists had even put up large coloured tents inscribed "Hotel", offering sleeping accommodation for the three days' duration of the festivities. For the peasants and nomads from outlying districts the annual gathering at Hemis is their golden opportunity of stocking up with vital necessities that they would otherwise have to go to Leh for.

Among the men in grey and wine-red cloaks I noticed several women wearing elaborate "Peraks", and Indian Civil Servants carving their way through the crowds. A little way off was a group of Lamas escorting a young boy tied to a small chair on a pony. As the procession passed slowly by I could see from his dark, childlike eyes how the long journey had wearied him. From his headgear it was clear that he belonged to the "Red Cap" sect, and in fact he was a reincarnation.

Another centre of attraction was the "Ling Khor", ("Ling" meaning garden and "Khor" ring), a park entirely surrounding the monastery. In it are hundreds of prayer-wheels, and the faithful are supposed to do their duty by them at least once a day, in the belief that the millions of prayers stored up in them will be duly wafted to their destination. Later, I saw in the monastery an enormous prayer-wheel which it takes two strong men just to move (page 80). Here inside the monastery the finishing touches were being put to the preparations. The butter-lamps had to be filled to overflowing as symbols of such an essentially joyous occasion, while the kitchens were

Deterrents: a figure wielding a bow and arrow hanging from the roof of a house in Alchi: A mummified dog fulfils a similar function in Rangdum Monastery. Below: the entrance to the abode of the spirits is guarded by a sheep's head hung with prayer-banners: while the monks of Ridzong Monastery are protected by a trident implanted in a skull.

147

working day and night to cater for monks making the pilgrimage from distant monasteries. Monks of an artistic turn of mind were busy fashioning curious cakes of dough, sugar and butter to be laid on the altars as "victual offerings", the butter having been previously coloured. Butter is also the principal ingredient of the artificial flowers and rosettes on the altars.

Next morning the festivities opened with a fanfare from the great trumpets in the temple. These huge instruments are several metres long, can be telescoped, and are made of copper with bands of silver along their immense length (page 153). Finally, the superb "thangka" portraying the founder of the monastery was unfurled on one of the monastery's walls (page 163).

The spectators massed on adjoining roofs, on balconies draped with brightly coloured hangings, on terraces, and in doorways were so densely packed that it was deemed advisable for Indian soldiers armed with truncheons to patrol the whole area but not to intervene except in an emergency.

The first group of performers to enter the courtyard were the celebrated "Black Hat" dancers (page 160), preceded by shawm-players and wearing brocade and silk costumes from China. On their breasts were death's-heads, and over them aprons made entirely of human bones (page 131, right). In their left hands they held bells, but instead of right hands, they brandished gruesome mummified arms bearing silver salvers for offerings.

During the intervals a Lama with a cloth over his mouth to keep out the dust kicked up by the dancers appeared with a beaker and a bottle of "chang" (Tibetan beer) which he sprinkled over the arena, a gesture symbolising the performers' resistance to the enemies of religion as well as reminding the spectators of the inevitability of death and of their dependance on the Lamas, who alone can ensure them a superior reincarnation.

It was late in the evening before the festivities came to an end, so we decided to leave it till the morrow before climbing up to the "eyrie", a retreat 4,000 metres above sea-level and the most sacred building at Hemis. Long before the completion of the great monastery the cave, above which a house has now been built, was inhabited by a hermit, and when it threatened to collapse during an earthquake he supported the roof on his broad shoulders, which is why the imprint of his body on the rock is still visible. Banknotes stuck to the walls by butter, and the hum of constant prayer, attest the pilgrims' veneration of this holy place.

At the entrance to the cave a monk was blowing a trumpet made out of a human thigh-bone studded with silver and precious stones. The thigh-bones are preferably those of criminals or victims of fatal accidents, as only trumpets made of such bones are powerful enough to invoke demons. I asked the monk whether there was anything worth seeing in the outlying buildings, but was told they were closed because some monks had immured themselves in them and taken a vow to refrain from speech for three years, three months and three days: they were living on barley-corn and butter-tea passed to them through a hole in the wall.

As I left the hermit's cave the monks were just beginning their prayers. They were celebrating an event that happens only once in a lifetime and that was therefore the highlight of the 1975 festivities, the induction of a reincarnation entitled "Drugpa Rinpoche", the spiritual head not only of Hemis but of the entire Drugpa sect, which is particularly widespread in Bhutan. The previous Rinpoche was a reincarnation who was being instructed in Tibet when the Chinese moved in. He was therefore deemed "missing" and the monastery was administered by the brother of the last King of Ladakh, but when after fifteen years there was still no news of the Rinpoche from Tibet, it was reluctantly decided to seek a new reincarnation, and eventually a 12 year old boy was discovered at Delhousie in India after his predecessor had been officially declared deceased in 1969. This procedure shows that the widely held view that the "new" Rinpoche must be born at the very moment the "old" one dies is erroneous. This was the boy who was now making his ceremonial entry into the precincts of Hemis to the festive sound of horns and trumpets.

Bearers of gifts formed themselves into a procession behind a group of monks who gently but firmly cleared a way for them through the crowd, and then amid an ear-splitting din the new "Drugpa Rinpoche" was escorted into the Great Hall, where he seated himself on a high throne behind a low table.

An incarnation is "discovered" by consulting oracles, by an interpretation of his precessor's last words, and by the application of various tests. The system not only ensures that the healthiest and most intelligent of the young "candidates" is selected but also eliminates the disadvantages of hereditary succession.

The 12-year old boy was accompanied by a haggard old man (an old acquaintance of mine) who is also a reincarnation; as "Baku Rinpoche" he was the elected member for the Province of Ladakh in the Indian Parliament until 1977.

The monks handed their new head ceremonial scarves, and in return were presented with similar scarves that had been blessed by the Rinpoche. After the Lamas, prominent lay figures were presented to him, and shortly afterwards, early in the afternoon, the Mystery Play began, watched by the 12-year old Rinpoche from his private box. The first players and dancers entered the courtyard preceded by an orchestra and monks with elaborate censers. Each group, each mask had its own special significance. The dancer with the bell and double-drum, for instance (page 161, below), symbolised the Buddhist religion. From time to time masked dancers mingled with the spectators (pages 150/151). The King of the Demons wore a dark-blue papier-mâché mask and could be identified by his third "Eye of Providence" (page 161, top left). More and more grotesquely masked figures came pouring into the arena, leaping and dancing in a hilarious parody of the conflict between good and evil. During the intervals monks handed round scarves blessed by the Drugpa Rinpoche (page 158/159). Players clad in rags and tatters represented departed souls wandering aimlessly in space in their search for some way out of the darkness, and every now and then they were joined by other groups representing local tutelary spirits; and so it went on hour after hour until the great trumpets (page 161, middle left) sounded the signal for the Finale to begin with figures representing good spirits, despite their terrifying masks, celebrating the victory of Buddhism over Shamanism. The saviours of true religion, warriors with triangular flags on their helmets and bells on their feet, represented the heroes who had succeeded in converting the evil demons to the Tibetan form of Buddhism. These demons had polluted the earth, the air and the waters, but they could not annihilate the human race. The triumph of good over evil was complete.

During an interval I was summoned by the Rinpoche: a monk on police duty had mistaken my identity in the crowd and hit me with a leather whip, so the Rinpoche wished to know whether I wanted the policeman punished. "Of course not", I replied. To the seething mass of people seeking the Rinpoche's blessing he held out his hand, but more important personages were presented with scarves to be worn round their necks as amulets.

The 12-year old Rinpoche, a good-natured and highly intelligent boy (page 167) bombarded me with questions, some of which I was unable to answer in the general hubbub, but I gave him a photograph of the Dalai Lama, which he immediately enclosed in a wrapping and placed on a nearby table alongside a bowl of dried apricots and a cup of tea.

Pages 150 and 151
*A group of players seated in front of the spectators are
wearing papier-mâché masks: the sharply contrasting
expressions are intended as comic representations of the
conflict between good and evil.*

→

*Monks sounding long copper trumpets signal the start of the
mystery play at Hemis Monastery. The trumpets can be
extended like telescopes.*

Pages 154/155
*"Stag-dancers": a leading part in the mystery play at Hemis
is enacted by a performer from Mongolia whom the author
had previously admired in Lhasa.*

Soldiers ancient and modern. While the former enact the conflict between good and evil, the latter (from India) ensure that the spectators do not get out of hand.

Players during an interval. A monk is bringing them "good-luck" scarves to be worn round the neck: the scarves have been blessed by the head of Hemis Monastery, the 12-years old Drugpa Rinpoche, and there is one for every performer. As well as a bell and a thunderbolt, the performers are holding Damaru drums.

Scenes from the Hemis mystery play: left, a "black hat" dancer. Right: masks intended to inspire terror, and monks making music.

Pages 162/163 Spectators seated on roofs, balconies and bridges decorated with banners in the ritual colours. They have been watching the Thangka banner, 3 metres by 6, being unrolled: it covers the entire frontage of a house.

The air-dried hand of the artist who painted the large Thangka on page 163. At the great festival this relic is carried by a special dancer.

The bowl and bottle of Tibetan beer this monk is holding are for the "black hat" dancer (page 160). The cloth covering the chin is to prevent contamination.

Page 165
A performer handling with great care a very precious antique pair of cymbals: their value depends on their pitch rather than on the metal they are made of.

A god in an official position: the 12-year-old Drugpa Rinpoche, the head of Hemis Monastery, receives the homage of the faithful with appropriate dignity. Below: He is invariably accompanied by his mentor, a sage of great wisdom.

A conversation in Tibetan: Well aware that the author was once the teacher of the Dalai Lama and is still his friend, Drugpa Rinpoche expressed a wish to enjoy a conversation with him. It was with a mixture of pride and reverence that the 12-year-old accepted a photograph of the author and the exiled Dalai Lama at Dharamshala in India.

The ceremony is over and Drugpa Rinpoche gets to his feet with a smile, glad to ease his stiff joints and muscles after sitting motionless for several hours.

Index

(Numbers referring to illustrations are medium-faced)

Bibliography:

Arora, Kashmir, Ladakh, Gilgit
Martin Brauen/Heinrich Harrers Impressionen aus Tibet
Crump, A Ride to Leh
A. Cunningham, Ladak
E. L. Datta, History of Ladakh
Deasy, In Tibet and Chinese Turkestan
Desideri/Freyre, Early Jesuite Travellers in Central Asia
Drews, Northern Barrier of India
Edair, Sport in Ladakh
A. H. Francke, A History of Western Tibet
  – Geistesleben in Tibet
  – Felszeichnungen aus Unter Ladakh
  – Some More Rock Carvings from Lower Ladakh
  – The Eighteen Songs of the Bono-Na Festival
  – Historische Dokumente von Khalatse in West-Tibet, Ladakh
  – Archeology in Western Tibet
  – Remarks on Stone Monuments near Ating in Zangskar
  – Ten Ancient Historical Songs from Western Tibet
  – Felsinschriften in Ladakh
  – Antiquities of Indian Tibet
B. Fraser, Journal of a Tour through Part of the Snowy Ranges of the Himalayan Mountains and the Sources of the Rivers Jamna and Ganges
M. Geary, Western Tibet
M. S. Gill, Himalayan Wonderland
H. Harrer, Sieben Jahre in Tibet
  – Geister und Dämonen
F. M. Hassnain, Buddhist Kashmir
F. M. Hassnain/Tokan D. Sumi/Masato Oti, Ladakh: The Moonland
A. Reeve + Kathleen M. Heber, Himalayan Tibet & Ladakh
Sven Hedin, Transhimalaya
Gerhard Heyde, Fünfzig Jahre unter Tibetern
Pierre Jaccard/Pierre Vittoz, Ladakh
A. Lamb, The China-India Border
C Lambert, Trip to Kashmir & Ladakh

D. I. Lauf, Zur Geschichte und Kunst lamaistischer Klöster im Westhimalaya
Heinz Lucas, Lamaistische Masken
K. Marx, History of Ladakh
Veen Mehta, Folk-Tales of Ladakh
Montgomery, Routes in Western Himalayas
W. Moorcroft/G. Trebeck, Travels in the Himalayan Provinces of Hindustan and the Punjab, in Ladakh and Kashmir etc.
J. C. Murray, Our Visit to Hindustan, Kashmir & Ladakh
A. Neve, Tourist Guide to Kashmir, Ladakh & Skardo
L. Petech, A Study of Chronicles of Ladakh
Friedrich A. Peter, Glossary of Place Names in Western Tibet
Swami Pranavananda, Exploration in Tibet
H. Ramsay, Western Tibet
S. H. Ribbach, Drogpa Namgyal
Margret und Rolf Schettler, Kaschmir und Ladakh
Hermann Schlagintweit-Sakünlunski, Reisen in Indien und Hochasien
Hermann und Robert Schlagintweit, Results of a Scientific Mission to India and High Asia
Ch. A. Sherring, Western Tibet and the British Borderland
M. Singh, Himalayan Art
D. Snellgrove/H. Richardson, A Cultural History of Tibet
Torrens, Travels in Ladakh, Tartary & Kashmir
G. M. Toscano, La Prima Missione Cattolica Nel Tibet
G. Tucci, Indo Tibetica
  – Tibetan Painted Scrolls
G. Tucci/E. Ghersi, Secrets of Tibet
Hashmat Ullah Khan, Tagebuch des Gouverneurs von Ladakh (1894–1936)
G. T. Vigne, Travels in Kashmir, Ladakh & Iskardu
L. A. Waddell, The Buddhism of Tibet or Lamaism
Ward, Sportsman Guide to Kashmir and Ladakh
T. V. Wylie, The Geography of Tibet